Fill three one-cup measuring cups with water. How many different cups of water are there? Pour them into a large bowl. There are three different cups of water in the bowl, but still there is only one bowl of water. That may help you understand how something can be three and one at the same time.

The persons

of God are perfectly united. They always agree. They have existed together forever. There is a special name for them. It is the "Trinity." There is nothing else like the Trinity. It is a very hard thing to understand—even for grownups. Just as you believe that your great-great-grandparents existed, you must also believe in the Trinity. The Bible says it's so, and that makes it true.

God's Word

The grace of the Lord Jesus Christ, the love of God, and the fellowship of the Holy Spirit be with you all.
2 CORINTHIANS 13:14

When all the people were being baptized by John, Jesus also was baptized. While Jesus was praying, heaven opened and the Holy Spirit came down on him. The Spirit was in the form of a dove. Then a voice came from heaven and said, "You are my Son and I love you. I am very pleased with you."
LUKE 3:21–22

So go and make followers of all people in the world. Baptize them in the name of the Father and the Son and the Holy Spirit.
MATTHEW 28:19

Listen, people of Israel! The Lord is our God. He is the only Lord.
DEUTERONOMY 6:4

SEE ALSO:
Matthew 5:48
John 1:1
Hebrews 1:8
1 Corinthians 2:11

What should we do when we don't understand God?

There is so much truth about God that we cannot understand. So, what should we do? The *wrong* thing is to doubt or ignore the truths that are too hard for us. That is what many people do. They reject the glory of God because they cannot understand it. They worship their own idols instead. An *idol* is a false god. Usually it is a small god with human features. Some people worship imaginary gods like animals or statues or things made of wood, stone, or metal. It is sinful to worship any man-made gods.

WORD SCRAMBLE

Question: How great is God?

TERGREA HANT YINGTHAN EW NAC GINEAMI

PRAYER STARTER

Dear God:
I won't lose faith when
I don't understand You.

Worship God today! Make up a song to praise Him or write a story or poem about how wonderful He is.

Your parents

are wiser than you are because they have lived longer. God is wiser than all humans not only because He has existed forever, but also because all true wisdom comes from God. It is right to worship God, because He is far greater and wiser than anything or anyone we could ever imagine. No wonder we cannot understand everything about Him! But that is a reason to praise God—and not a reason to doubt Him.

God's Word

Yes, God's riches are very great! God's wisdom and knowledge have no end! No one can explain the things God decides. No one can understand God's ways. As the Scripture says, "Who has known the mind of the Lord? Who has been able to give the Lord advice? No one has ever given God anything that he must pay back." Yes, God made all things. And everything continues through God and for God. To God be the glory forever!
ROMANS 11:33-36

"We are God's children. So, you must not think that God is like something that people imagine or make. He is not like gold, silver, or rock."
ACTS 17:29

SEE ALSO:
Daniel 5:23
Exodus 20:3-5
Romans 1:22-23

What can we understand about God?

There is much about God that we *can* understand. For example, everything about Him is good. There is not one thing about Him that is evil. God is *holy*. He is *perfectly* holy. He is the Creator of everything. God made everything that exists. He has the right to rule everything. He is Lord over everything. God is a God of love. Everything He commands us to do is good. Therefore, we know that He deserves our love, obedience, and worship. These are truths about God that are not too hard for us to understand.

WORD SCRAMBLE

Question: How much should we love God?

REMO HANT YINGTHAN RO ONEYNA SEEL

Answer: More than anything or anyone else

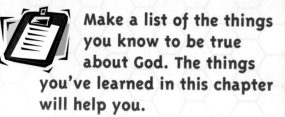

Make a list of the things you know to be true about God. The things you've learned in this chapter will help you.

LOOK

at the wonderful things God has made! You can't understand *all* of them, but you *can* know enough to worship God, and you can praise Him forever. Some things about God will be impossible for you to understand, but you can understand *enough* to know you should love Him more than anything or anyone else. He has revealed enough for you to know Him in a personal way. You cannot understand everything about God completely, but you can trust Him and believe everything His Word says about Him—even the things you don't understand.

God's Word

You know that God has sent his message to the people of Israel. That message is the Good News that peace has come through Jesus Christ. Jesus is the Lord of all people!
ACTS 10:36

Whoever does not love does not know God, because God is love.
1 JOHN 4:8

Loving God means obeying his commands. And God's commands are not too hard for us.
1 JOHN 5:3

Here is the message we have heard from God and now tell to you: God is light, and in him there is no darkness at all.
1 JOHN 1:5

SEE ALSO:
Isaiah 6:3

CHAPTER 2

Creation

REPORT CARD

A+

Has God really lived forever?

In the very beginning, there was nothing but God. There was no time. There was no space. There was nothing to touch. There was nothing and no one to see or hear. Only the Father, the Son, and the Holy Spirit existed. There was no sky or earth. There were no animals and no people. There was no one but God Himself to enjoy His perfect glory.

God made the universe and all His creatures so He could put His perfect glory on display. All creation

shows His wisdom, His power, and His goodness. And when history is finished, those who love God will live with Him in heaven and enjoy His glory forever.

WORD SCRAMBLE

Question: What existed in the beginning?

THINGON TUB ODG

Answer: Nothing but God

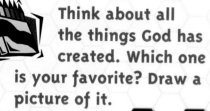

Think about all the things God has created. Which one is your favorite? Draw a picture of it.

Can you

imagine living without beautiful summer days? Without your pets? Without the moon and the stars? All of those things are the blessings of God's creation. His creation is a wonderful blessing that He shares with us. We should be grateful that He made us and gave us life. And our lives should always glorify Him.

God's Word

[Jesus prayed] "And now, Father, give me glory with you. Give me the glory I had with you before the world was made."
JOHN 17:5

The heavens tell the glory of God. And the skies announce what his hands have made.
PSALM 19:1

I heard a loud voice from the throne. The voice said, "Now God's home is with men. He will live with them, and they will be his people. God himself will be with them and will be their God. He will wipe away every tear from their eyes. There will be no more death, sadness, crying, or pain. All the old ways are gone."
REVELATION 21:3-4

How long did it take God to create the universe?

Did you know that God created the whole universe in just six days? Can you imagine the power it took to create so much—and in such a short time?

Next time you look at the stars at night, think about how big the universe is. There are far too many stars to count. And even the closest ones are so far away that you could never travel there in your whole lifetime. God made it all! And it took Him only six days.

PRAYER STARTER

Dear God:
Thank You for Your wonderful creation.

WORD SCRAMBLE

Question: How long did it take God to create the universe?

ODG TREACED HET SERVEIUN NI IXS YADS.

Answer: God created the universe in six days.

Is there a construction site near where you live? See how much the workers can get done in one day. Then imagine God creating the universe in only six days!

God's Word

Before the world began, there was the Word. The Word was with God, and the Word was God.
JOHN 1:1

God looked at everything he had made, and it was very good.
GENESIS 1:31

"God is in the highest part of heaven. See how high the highest stars are!"
JOB 22:12

The Lord does great things. Those people who love them think about them.
PSALM 111:2

OUR sun is a very small star. All the other stars you see in the sky are much bigger than the sun. But they are so far away that they look tiny. Some of the "stars" are really large galaxies that have hundreds and thousands of stars in them. No matter how big you imagine the universe, it is much bigger than you think. And God made it all!

What happened on the first day?

The Bible tells us what happened in the six days of creation. On the first day, God created the heavens and the earth. At first, the earth was dark and empty. And then He created light. God created everything without any effort. He just gave a command, and the heavens and earth appeared. Then He gave another command, and the light appeared. He divided the light from the darkness to make day and night. And that was the first day ever.

PRAYER STARTER

Dear God:
Thank You for creating night and day.

WORD SCRAMBLE

Question: What did God create on the first day?

HET SVENHEA DAN ETH REATH

Answer: The heavens and the earth

When it is dark outside, take a flashlight into the darkest room of your house. Imagine what it would be like if the earth were dark all the time. Then turn the flashlight on. It was easier for God to create light than it was for you to turn on the flashlight.

Everything

that God did, He did without any effort at all. It was easy for Him. He just commanded it to be done—and it happened! Can you imagine commanding your room to be clean or commanding your homework to be done perfectly?

God's Word

In the beginning God created the sky and the earth. The earth was empty and had no form. Darkness covered the ocean, and God's Spirit was moving over the water. Then God said, "Let there be light!" And there was light. God saw that the light was good. So he divided the light from the darkness. God named the light "day" and the darkness "night." Evening passed, and morning came. This was the first day.
GENESIS 1:1–5

What happened on the second day?

On the second day, God formed the earth's sky, and He gave our planet the air we breathe. He also separated the water on the earth from the clouds in the sky. That was the second day.

WORD SCRAMBLE

Question: What did God create on the second day?

EHT IRA DAN HET KYS

Answer: The air and the sky

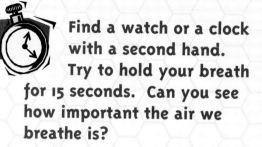

Find a watch or a clock with a second hand. Try to hold your breath for 15 seconds. Can you see how important the air we breathe is?

God's Word

Then God said, "Let there be something to divide the water in two!" So God made the air to divide the water in two. Some of the water was above the air, and some of the water was below it. God named the air "sky." Evening passed, and morning came. This was the second day.

GENESIS 1:6-8

Have you

seen pictures of astronauts walking on the moon? They had tanks of oxygen on their backs so they could breathe. God knew that the animals and people He would create on earth would need air to breathe, so He gave our planet oxygen. He knew that we would be thirsty, so He created water for us to drink. Everything God did was perfect.

What happened on the third day?

On the third day, God gathered all the water on the earth into oceans. Dry land appeared for the first time. Then God created all kinds of plants, grass, and trees. Those were the first living things on earth.

WORD SCRAMBLE

Question: What did God create on the third day?

NEASCO NAD SPLATN

Answer: Oceans and plants

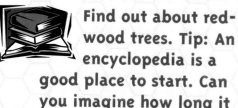

Find out about red-wood trees. Tip: An encyclopedia is a good place to start. Can you imagine how long it would take for a redwood tree to grow as high as it can be? God could create one instantly!

Have you

ever planted a seed and waited for it to grow? It took a long time for that seed to sprout, didn't it? But when God commanded the earth to have plants, trees, and grass— it just happened. He didn't have to wait for them to grow, like you and I do. That's because God is so great. The things He does are greater than anything we can imagine.

God's Word

Then God said, "Let the water under the sky be gathered together so the dry land will appear." And it happened. God named the dry land "earth." He named the water that was gathered together "seas." God saw that this was good. Then God said, "Let the earth produce plants. Some plants will make grain for seeds. Others will make fruit with seeds in it. Every seed will produce more of its own kind of plant." And it happened. The earth produced plants. Some plants had grain for seeds. The trees made fruit with seeds in it. Each seed grew its own kind of plant. God saw that all this was good. Evening passed, and morning came. This was the third day.
GENESIS 1:9–13

What happened on the fourth day?

On the fourth day, God made all the stars. He also made the sun and the moon. He had already created light on the first day. The Bible doesn't say where the light came from for those first three days, but God somehow caused light to shine on the earth in the daytime. But after the fourth day, all the daylight on the earth came from the sun. And the moon and stars gave the earth light at night.

WORD SCRAMBLE

Question: What did God create on the fourth day?

HET NUS, NOMO, DAN RATSS

Answer: The sun, moon, and stars

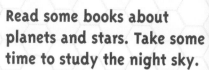

Read some books about planets and stars. Take some time to study the night sky. Some stars together look like certain things, for example a bear or a cooking pot. Can you imagine God making all those stars in just one day?

God's Word

Then God said, "Let there be lights in the sky to separate day from night. These lights will be used for signs, seasons, days and years. They will be in the sky to give light to the earth." And it happened. So God made the two large lights. He made the brighter light to rule the day. He made the smaller light to rule the night. He also made the stars. God put all these in the sky to shine on the earth. They are to rule over the day and over the night. He put them there to separate the light from the darkness. God saw that all these things were good. Evening passed, and morning came. This was the fourth day.

GENESIS 1:14–19

The stars and the space they cover are far greater than we could ever imagine. The sun is our closest star. It is so large that if it were a hollow ball, a million planets the size of the earth would fit into it. Yet the sun is small compared to other stars. (It just looks bigger because it is so much closer to earth.) There are billions of stars. Many are too far away to be visible on earth. But God can see them all. He made them for His pleasure. You can see how God is greater than anything we could ever see or imagine. We should praise Him for His greatness.

What happened on the fifth day?

On the fifth day, God created all the fish and whales and the living creatures in the oceans. He also made birds to fill the sky with life.

God was pleased with the birds and fish and living creatures in the ocean and blessed them all. He told them to have many young ones and grow in number.

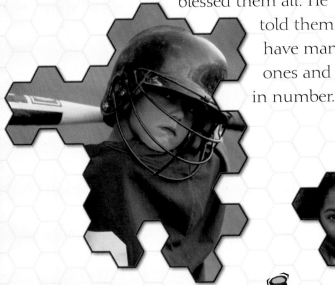

WORD SCRAMBLE

Question: What did God create on the fifth day?

HET SHIF DAN HET DRIBS

nswer: The fish and the birds

 How many different kinds of birds are there? A field guide to birds will give you an idea. Tip: You can find a field guide at the library. Can you imagine how great God must be to have created so many different kinds of birds?

Have you

ever seen flocks of geese flying through the sky? It's a very awesome thing. There can be more of them than you can count. They make so much noise that you can hear them even when you are inside your house. Can you imagine what it was like on the fifth day when God created all of the birds? What a sight that must have been!

God's Word

Then God said, "Let the water be filled with living things. And let birds fly in the air above the earth." So God created the large sea animals. He created every living thing that moves in the sea. The sea is filled with these living things. Each one produces more of its own kind. God also made every bird that flies. And each bird produces more of its own kind. God saw that this was good. God blessed them and said, "Have many young ones and grow in number. Fill the water of the seas, and let the birds grow in number on the earth." Evening passed, and morning came. This was the fifth day.
GENESIS 1:20-23

What happened on the sixth day?

On the sixth day, God made all the animals to live on the dry land. He made everything from insects to large animals. He made spiders, snakes, dogs, cows, and every other kind of animal.

God told them to all have many babies. Soon, all kinds of wild animals, tame animals, and small crawling animals filled the earth.

WORD SCRAMBLE

Question: What did God create on the sixth day?

LAL EHT MALANSI

PRAYER STARTER

Dear God:
Thank You for creating all the animals.

What is your favorite animal? Create it from clay or draw a picture of it. How much time did it take you to do that? Imagine—God created ALL the animals in just one day.

A ZOO

is the only place where you are likely to see many different kinds of animals. Some of them live in trees and some live underground. Some are awake in the daytime and sleep at night. Some are awake at night and sleep in the daytime. God made thousands of different kinds of animals. He knew before He created them just where they would live and what they would need.

God's Word

Then God said, "Let the earth be filled with animals. And let each produce more of its own kind. Let there be tame animals and small crawling animals and wild animals. And let each produce more of its kind." And it happened. So God made the wild animals, the tame animals and all the small crawling animals to produce more of their own kind. God saw that this was good.
GENESIS 1:24-25

How did God create men?

Everything God had made so far, He made out of nothing, simply by giving a command. When He said, "Sun!" the sun appeared. And when He said "Fish!" all the fish appeared. God is so powerful that He can create anything He wants just by saying it.

Before the sixth day ended, God made the first man. Man was a special creature, not like any of the others. So instead of speaking the word and creating him out of nothing, God formed him from the dust of the earth. Then He breathed life into him.

PRAYER STARTER
Dear God:
Thank You for creating dads, grandfathers, uncles, sons, and brothers.

WORD SCRAMBLE

Question: Besides the animals, what did God create on the sixth day?

OGD RETACED A ANM.

Answer: God created a man.

At the top of a piece of paper, write your name and the name of your pet or a favorite animal. Write down five things that both you and your pet can do. Now write ten things that you can do but your pet can't.

GOD made man to be different from all the other living things. Look around you. There is not one other living thing that is just like you. God made you different from the animals and plants He created. Animals and plants can't solve hard problems. They can't write stories, draw pictures, or sing the words to a song. They can't appreciate all the beautiful things that God created. God gave man special abilities because He created man in His own image.

God's Word

Then the Lord God took dust from the ground and formed man from it. The Lord breathed the breath of life into the man's nose. And the man became a living person.
GENESIS 2:7

I look at the heavens, which you made with your hands. I see the moon and stars, which you created. But why is man important to you? Why do you take care of human beings? You made man a little lower than the angels. And you crowned him with glory and honor. You put him in charge of everything you made. You put all things under his control: all the sheep, the cattle and the wild animals, the birds in the sky, the fish in the sea, and everything that lives under water. Lord our Master, your name is the most wonderful name in all the earth!
PSALM 8:3–8

SEE ALSO:
Psalm 100:3
Genesis 9:66-7

How did God create women?

God created a woman to be the man's wife, and He used a special method. He caused the man to fall asleep. Then He removed some bone and flesh from the man's side. From that bone and flesh, God made the first woman. He named the man Adam. And Adam named his wife Eve. Every person who has ever lived came from that first family.

PRAYER STARTER

Dear God:
Thank You for creating moms, grandmothers, daughters, aunts, and sisters.

WORD SCRAMBLE

Question: Along with the animals and man, what else did God create on the sixth day?

ODG TEDAECR A NOWAM.

Answer: God created a woman.

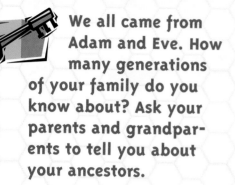

We all came from Adam and Eve. How many generations of your family do you know about? Ask your parents and grandparents to tell you about your ancestors.

WHEN GOD

created the animals, He made sure to create more than one of each kind. It was a part of His perfect plan. And when He created man, He also created another human—woman—so that the man would not be alone and so they could be fathers and mothers. Whatever God does, He does it because it is best for us. And He always does it in a *perfect* way.

God's Word

God took one of the ribs from the man's body. Then God closed the man's skin at the place where he took the rib. The Lord God used the rib from the man to make a woman. Then the Lord brought the woman to the man.
GENESIS 2:21–22

The man named his wife Eve. This is because she is the mother of everyone who ever lived.
GENESIS 3:20

Were Adam and Eve just like God?

The Bible tells us that God created Adam and Eve in His image. Remember—that doesn't mean they looked like God, because He is an invisible Spirit. But they were like God in other ways. They were able to love like God. (They could love God and love each other.) They were able to think about things the way God does. And Adam and Eve were able to be creative. The first creative thing Adam did was name all God's creatures.

WORD SCRAMBLE

Question: What was the first creative thing Adam did?

MADA MANED LAL HET RESTUEARC.

Answer: Adam named all the creatures.

If you could have any pet in the world, what would it be? Think hard about what you would name it and why. Can you imagine Adam having to name ALL the different animals?

GOD put Adam and Eve in charge of all the earth. He placed them in a garden where they had all the food they wanted. It was a perfect garden in a perfect world. You are like Adam and Eve in many ways. You are greater than all of the plants and animals, and it is your job to take care of them.

God's Word

So God created human beings in his image. In the image of God he created them. He created them male and female.
GENESIS 1:27

From the ground God formed every wild animal and every bird in the sky. He brought them to the man so the man could name them. Whatever the man called each living thing, that became its name. The man gave names to all the tame animals, to the birds in the sky and to all the wild animals.
GENESIS 2:19-20

What happened on the seventh day?

God looked over all His creation. Everything was *very* good. So on the seventh day, God rested from creating. That doesn't mean He was tired. But He was finished with all His creative work. In just six days, He had made everything in the universe, and He had made it perfectly. God was very, very pleased with everything He had made.

It was a world without sin. The whole world was filled with nothing but good things. There was no sickness. There was no bad weather. It was never too hot or too cold. It was a perfect place for Adam and Eve.

WORD SCRAMBLE

Question: What did God do on the seventh day?

ODG STERED.

Answer: God rested.

Take some time to rest today. And while you're resting, think about the Creation. Think about how much God did in only SIX days.

THINGS

did not stay perfect for long. Soon Adam and Eve disobeyed God, and that was the beginning of all the trouble in the world. When you disobey, does it ever lead to anything good? Disobedience is sin, and sin ruins everything. You know that—and Adam and Eve found that out, too.

God's Word

By the seventh day God finished the work he had been doing. So on the seventh day he rested from all his work.
GENESIS 2:2

In six days the Lord made everything. He made the sky, earth, sea and everything in them. And on the seventh day, he rested. So the Lord blessed the Sabbath day and made it holy.
EXODUS 20:11

Sin

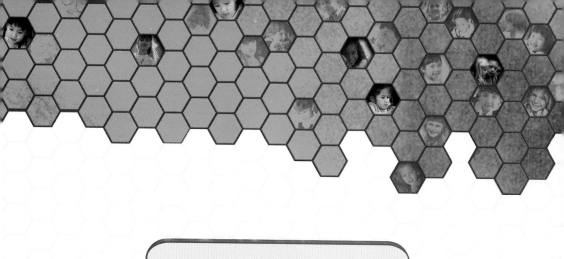

The story of how sin started

When God put Adam and Eve in the garden, He gave them only one rule—they were not to eat from the tree in the middle of the garden. They could eat the fruit from any *other* tree—just not the one in the middle. All the food they needed was in the garden. Adam and Eve could eat anything, except the fruit from that *one* tree.

God commanded Adam to take care of the garden. It wasn't hard for Adam to do, because there were no weeds in that garden and nothing to hurt the plants. Everything was perfect, and taking care of the garden was pure joy.

There was no sickness, hunger, worry, or pain in the garden. As long as Adam and Eve obeyed that one rule, they would live there forever and they would never die.

Then, one day, something terrible happened. A serpent spoke to Eve in the garden. The snake was really Satan in disguise. (Satan is an angel who fought against God and became evil.) The snake tricked Eve into eating the forbidden fruit. He told her that she and Adam would be as wise as God if they ate it. But God had said that if they ate from that tree they would die. Satan said God lied, and they wouldn't die.

Eve thought that the snake was telling her the truth, so she ate the fruit. And Adam ate it, too. As soon as they ate it, they died. They didn't drop dead to the ground, but they died in spirit—that means that the perfect joy they had known was gone.

God sent Adam and Eve out of the garden. All the perfect things were gone. Adam and Eve had to work, just like we do. Their bodies would grow old, and some day they would die, just as we will.

God's Word

The Lord God put the man in the garden of Eden to care for it and work it. The Lord God commanded him, "You may eat the fruit from any tree in the garden. But you must not eat the fruit from the tree which gives the knowledge of good and evil. If you ever eat fruit from that tree, you will die!"

GENESIS 2:15-17

Now the snake was the most clever of all the wild animals the Lord God had made. One day the snake spoke to the woman. He said, "Did God really say that you must not eat fruit from any tree in the garden?" The woman answered the snake, "We may eat fruit from the trees in the garden. But God told us, 'You must not eat from the tree that is in the middle of the garden. You must not even touch it, or you will die.'"

GENESIS 3:1-3

But the snake said to the woman, "You will not die. God knows that if you eat the fruit from that tree, you will learn about good and evil. Then you will be like God!"

GENESIS 3:4-5

Then God said to the man, "You listened to what your wife said. And you ate fruit from the tree that I commanded you not to eat from. So I will put a curse on the ground. You will have to work very hard for food. In pain you will eat its food all the days of your life. The ground will produce thorns and weeds for you. And you will eat the plants of the field. You will sweat and work hard for your food. Later you will return to the ground. This is because you were taken from the ground. You are dust. And when you die, you will return to the dust."

GENESIS 3:17-19

SEE ALSO:
Genesis 3:8-10
Genesis 3:16
Genesis 3:23

What makes us sin today?

All of us are like Adam and Eve. Except for Jesus, every person who has ever been born into this world has been born with the same love for sin. Some people may seem worse than others, but the truth is that all of us sin. We choose to do things that are wrong, even though we know we shouldn't.

Have you ever noticed that sometimes when we know we are not supposed to do something, we only want to do it more? Often, we do wrong things just because we know we shouldn't. That's just like Adam and Eve, isn't it?

WORD SCRAMBLE

Question: Who are we like?

DAMA DAN VEE

PRAYER STARTER

Dear God:
I want to obey You.

Answer: Adam and Eve

What is your most favorite treat? Imagine that it's there in front of you right now. Imagine that you could never taste it again. What would you do? Try it for real sometime.

THERE WAS

only one thing in the garden that Adam and Eve couldn't eat, but they ate it anyway! What would you have done if you were in their place? Have you wanted something you were told you couldn't have? Just like Adam and Eve, all of us can be tempted to do things that are wrong.

God's Word

You might think that I am saying that sin and the law are the same thing. That is not true. But the law was the only way I could learn what sin meant. I would never have known what it means to want something wrong if the law had not said, "You must not want to take your neighbor's things." And sin found a way to use that command and cause me to want every kind of wrong thing. So sin came to me because of that command. But without the law, sin has no power.
ROMANS 7:7-8

All people have sinned and are not good enough for God's glory.
ROMANS 3:23

What has sin done to our world?

When God created the world, everything was perfect and good. There was no sin—none at all! But once sin came into the world, nothing was perfect anymore. Everything that is wrong with the world is because of sin. Sickness, suffering, pain, sorrow, weakness, earthquakes, floods, fighting, wars, divorce, drugs, crime, fear, hate, murder, death, and all other sad and bad things are everywhere in our world because of sin. Sin is the most terrible thing in our lives. It ruined the whole universe, and it will ruin all of us, unless we are forgiven.

God knew that all of us would be sinners, so He sent Jesus to die for our sins. Jesus was punished in our place so that we could be forgiven.

WORD SCRAMBLE

Question: What can we do to be forgiven for our sins?

EW NAC KAS GDO OT VIEGROF SU.

Answer: We can ask God to forgive us.

Write a letter to God. Tell Him that you're sorry for your sins, and ask Him to forgive you.

Can you

imagine a perfect world, a place where everything is good, a place where no bad things happen and where there are no sickness and no pain? That is what God wants for us, and that is what's waiting for us in heaven. Everyone sins—your pastor, your parents, your teacher, your friends. But the good news is that God will forgive you for your sins. That's because Jesus was punished in your place. If you tell God that you're sorry for your sins and ask Him to forgive you, then you will be forgiven.

God's Word

As the Scriptures say: "There is no one without sin. None! There is no one who understands. There is no one who looks to God for help. . . . " All people have sinned and are not good enough for God's glory.
ROMANS 3:10–11, 23

When someone sins, he earns what sin pays—death. But God gives us a free gift—life forever in Christ Jesus our Lord.
ROMANS 6:23

Everything that God made was changed to become useless. This was not by its own wish. It happened because God wanted it. But there was this hope: that everything God made . . . would have the freedom and glory that belong to God's children. We know that everything God made has been waiting until now in pain, like a woman ready to give birth.
ROMANS 8:20–22

Can God tell us what to do?

In the Bible, God has given us many commands. They show us what is right. They show us what pleases Him. Here is one of them: "Children, obey your parents."

That is a simple commandment. It is almost as simple as the commandment God gave Adam. Have you ever broken the commandment to obey your parents? I know you have because all of us have. The Bible says we are all sinners. We find it impossible to obey God perfectly. We cannot even obey our *parents* perfectly, and that is easier than obeying God.

PRAYER STARTER

Dear God:
Help me to do what is right.

WORD SCRAMBLE

Question: How can we please God?

YB YINGOBE SIH DEMANTSONCMM

Answer: By obeying His commandments

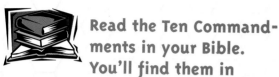

Read the Ten Commandments in your Bible. You'll find them in Deuteronomy 5:1-22. Think about what each of them means. Then try to memorize all of them.

THERE are more commands. For example: God wants us to love our neighbors the same way we love ourselves. The commands in the Bible teach us what we should think, how we should treat people, and what we should do. God wants us to obey all His commands perfectly. But we cannot. Because God is perfect, He cannot be pleased by what is imperfect. (If anything less pleased Him, He would not be perfect.) So, every time you disobey your parents or fight with a friend or act selfishly, you are not pleasing God. He is displeased every time you sin.

God's Word

Children, obey your parents the way the Lord wants. This is the right thing to do.
EPHESIANS 6:1

Honor your father and your mother. Then you will live a long time in the land. The Lord your God is going to give you this land.
EXODUS 20:12

"And the second command is like the first: 'Love your neighbor as you love yourself.'"
MATTHEW 22:39

All people have sinned and are not good enough for God's glory.
ROMANS 3:23

SEE ALSO:
Romans 6:23
Ezekiel 18:4
Revelation 20:10-14

What happens when we sin?

Nobody likes to talk about punishment, but every sin must be punished. Otherwise, God would be unfair. Sin is a very serious thing. Just *one* sin is as bad as breaking *every one* of God's commands.

We cannot make sin or punishment go away by trying to behave better. Feeling sorry about our sin does not make it go away, either. We cannot do what pleases God all the time; and we cannot fix our own sin.

We all have sinned *many* times. Everyone who has ever lived, except Jesus, has disobeyed God's commandments. We all deserve to be punished, and God would be perfectly right to punish us forever. But instead, He made a way to forgive us. He tells us about His gift of forgiveness and eternal life in the Bible—and it is very good news.

WORD SCRAMBLE

Question: What is God's special gift to anyone who trusts Him?

EARNETL FILE

Answer: Eternal life

PRAYER STARTER

Dear God:
Thank You for Your gift of eternal life.

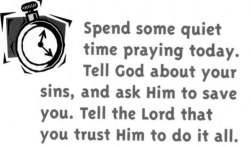

Spend some quiet time praying today. Tell God about your sins, and ask Him to save you. Tell the Lord that you trust Him to do it all.

The GOOD NeWs

is that God gives eternal life as a gift to anyone who trusts Him. When your parents punish you for doing wrong, it helps you learn to be obedient to them and to God, but it does not fix the wrong things you have already done. God doesn't want us to try to fix our own sins. Instead, *He* will do everything that needs to be done to save us from sin. God wants us to trust Him and Him alone to save us.

God's Word

A person might follow all of God's law. But if he fails to obey even one command, he is guilty of breaking all the commands in that law.
JAMES 2:10

Happy is the person whose sins are forgiven, whose wrongs are pardoned.
PSALM 32:1

Bible

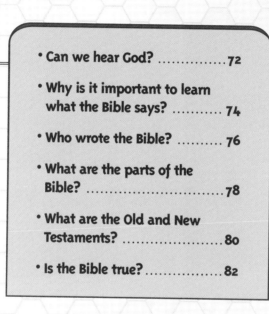

Can we hear God?

Do you know that God speaks to us? Not in a voice we hear with our ears, but in a book He has written— it's called the Bible.

You might think that the Bible is too big a book for you to read. Parts of it seem very hard to understand at first. But that's why God commands us to memorize it and think about it all the time.

The verses under "God's Word" on these pages are all from the Bible. Most of them are not hard to understand. If you understand them, then you are understanding the Bible.

PRAYER STARTER

Dear God:
Thank You for giving us the Bible.

WORD SCRAMBLE

Question: How can we hear God?

URHGOT HET DROWS NI HET LIBBE

Answer: Through the words in the Bible

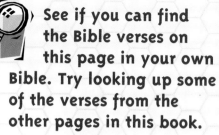

See if you can find the Bible verses on this page in your own Bible. Try looking up some of the verses from the other pages in this book.

Read your Bible a little at a time. Soon you will begin to understand it even better. The more you understand it, the more you will know about God. The Bible is His message to us. It tells us what He wants us to be like. It tells us what He wants us to do. Reading the Bible is our way of hearing what God has to say.

God's Word

Always remember what is written in the Book of the Teachings. Study it day and night. Then you will be sure to obey everything that is written there. If you do this, you will be wise and successful in everything.
JOSHUA 1:8

The Lord's teachings are perfect. They give new strength. The Lord's rules can be trusted. They make plain people wise.
PSALM 19:7

But women will be saved through having children. They will be saved if they continue in faith, love, holiness, and self-control.
1 TIMOTHY 2:15

As newborn babies want milk, you should want the pure and simple teaching. By it you can grow up and be saved.
1 PETER 2:2

Why is it important to learn what the Bible says?

The Bible is *full* of truth. You can spend your whole life studying it, and it still will be fresh and wonderful. It is the most important book in the whole world. In the Bible, God tells us what He is like. He tells us what He wants us to do. He shows us the way to eternal life. God tells us everything we need to know to please Him.

WORD SCRAMBLE

Question: What is the Bible filled with?

EHT LIBBE SI DILLEF THWI RUHTT.

Answer: The Bible is filled with truth.

PRAYER STARTER

Dear God:
I want to know all
about You.

 **The Bible begins with Genesis. Find Genesis in your Bible. Then read the first three chapters. Is this a story that you already know?**

God's Word

All Scripture is given by God and is useful for teaching and for showing people what is wrong in their lives. It is useful for correcting faults and teaching how to live right. Using the Scriptures, the person who serves God will be ready and will have everything he needs to do every good work.

2 TIMOTHY 3:16–17

SEE ALSO:
2 Peter 1:21

THE WHOLE BIBLE

is from God. All the important things God wants us to know are in the Bible. Every word in it is true. It is as if God Himself had written it down instead of using men to write it. That is why we should learn what the Bible says. It is very important to read it every single day. How often do you read your Bible?

Who wrote the Bible?

The Bible is more than just a big book. It is made up of sixty-six smaller books. Every one is a message from God. All the books of the Bible were written by men whom God chose to write His message for Him—men like Moses, Samuel, David, Matthew, John, Paul, Peter, and many others.

Many different men in many different times and places wrote the Bible, but they all agreed. The message of the Bible is the same from beginning to end. The Bible is much more than just what those men thought and said. The words are the words God chose. So God Himself is speaking to us in the Bible. That is why we call it "God's Word."

WORD SCRAMBLE

Question: What is another name for the Bible?

SODG ROWD

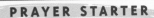

Answer: God's Word

The Bible is made up of sixty-six smaller books. Look in your Bible and see if you can find them all. Write the name of each one as you find it.

Can you

imagine a person living thousands of years ago, in a faraway place—someone you never met— writing the same message that you might write today? That's how it was with Moses, David, John, Paul, and the other men who wrote the Bible. They had never met one another, but they wrote about the same things. That's because God guided every word that they wrote.

God's Word

No prophecy ever came from what a man wanted to say. But men led by the Holy Spirit spoke words from God.
2 PETER 1:21

In the past God spoke to our ancestors through the prophets. He spoke to them many times and in many different ways.
HEBREWS 1:1

SEE ALSO:
2 Timothy 3:16–17

What are the parts of the Bible?

The Bible is made up of different parts. *History* tells about what happened from Creation on. *Law* tells about God's commands. It teaches what pleases and displeases God and shows us our sin. *Poetry* tells how to praise God. *Prophecy* tells about what God will do in the future. It says that He will destroy evil and make everything good again. Some prophecies have already come to pass. For example, long before Jesus was born, the Bible said He would be born in Bethlehem. And He was!

The Bible teaches us how to be wise, how to think, and how to treat one another. It teaches everything that is important to God and for us. But the main message of the Bible is about Jesus. It tells how He made it possible for us to be forgiven of all our sins forever.

WORD SCRAMBLE

Question: What are the parts of the Bible?

ROTSHIY, AWL, YROPHECP, DAN TRYOPE

Answer: History, Law, Prophecy, and Poetry

Plant a seed and watch it grow. Imagine God's Word growing inside your heart.

GOD'S WORD

is alive and powerful. That doesn't mean it is alive like a person. It means the Bible has the power to give us spiritual life. It tells us things we couldn't know any other way. It shows us the way to eternal life. The Bible is like a seed that has life in it. When it gets into our hearts, it springs to life inside us. It restores the spiritual life we lost because of sin. That's what makes it the most important book in the world.

God's Word

God's word is alive and working. It is sharper than a sword sharpened on both sides. It cuts all the way into us, where the soul and the spirit are joined. It cuts to the center of our joints and our bones. And God's word judges the thoughts and feelings in our hearts.
HEBREWS 4:12

You have been born again. This new life did not come from something that dies, but from something that cannot die. You were born again through God's living message that continues forever.
1 PETER 1:23

SEE ALSO:
1 Peter 2:2
Micah 5:2

What are the Old and New Testaments?

The first thirty-nine books of the Bible are called the *Old Testament*. The Old Testament was written long before Jesus came. The last twenty-seven books of the Bible are called the *New Testament*. The New Testament tells about Jesus' birth and everything He did. It tells how the church began and spread through the world through the teaching of Jesus' followers.

The Old Testament said Jesus would come and die to pay the penalty for other people's sin. It even predicted the very words Jesus would say when He died on the cross. Many things about Jesus were recorded in the Old Testament hundreds of years before He was even born. That is one of the ways we know the Bible is God's Word, because only God knows the future.

PRAYER STARTER
Dear God:
There is nothing that
You do not know.

WORD SCRAMBLE

Question: What are the two main parts of the Bible?

ETH DOL TASTETEMN DAN HET EWN STATENETM

Answer: The Old Testament and the New Testament

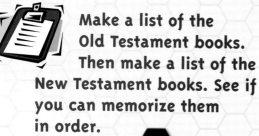

Make a list of the Old Testament books. Then make a list of the New Testament books. See if you can memorize them in order.

Many of the Old Testament's prophecies have come true. For example, one prophecy in the book of Daniel told about four great kingdoms that would rule the world. It happened exactly the way God said it would. Everything that you see happening today is happening just as God knew it would. There is nothing that He does not know. Everything is a part of His perfect plan.

God's Word

He said to them, "Remember when I was with you before? I said that everything written about me must happen—everything in the law of Moses, the books of the prophets, and the Psalms."
LUKE 24:44

"Another kingdom will come after you. But that kingdom will not be as great as yours. Next a third kingdom will rule over the earth. That is the bronze part. Then there will be a fourth kingdom, strong as iron. Iron crushes and smashes things to pieces. In the same way the fourth kingdom will smash and crush all the other kingdoms."
DANIEL 2:39–40

SEE ALSO:
Isaiah 53:4–5
Psalm 22:1
Matthew 27:46
Ezekiel 26:4–5

Is the Bible true?

We know the Bible is really the Word of God because many prophecies have already come true. We also know that the history in the Bible is true. People who study the ruins of old cities have found that what the Bible tells us about them is always right.

The best way to know that the Bible is true is by the way it changes our lives when we believe it and study it. Millions of lives have been changed because of the Bible. When people believe the Bible and follow what it says, they come alive spiritually. The Bible gives them a love for God. It changes their lives for good. Best of all, it shows them the way to eternal life.

WORD SCRAMBLE

Question: What does the Bible show us?

ETH AWY OT LEARNET FILE

PRAYER STARTER

Dear God:
I believe that the Bible
will change my life.

What have you learned about the Bible? Write a story about it. Share your story with a friend.

The ONLY way

to know God and to be free from the effects of our sin is to *believe* that the Bible is true. The *proof* that the Bible is true is that it really does change people's lives. Try it. Study your Bible every day and believe what it says. I know the Bible is true because God has used it to change my life. How about you?

God's Word

The one who reads the words of God's message is happy. And the people who hear this message and do what is written in it are happy. The time is near when all of this will happen.
REVELATION 1:3

Your word is like a lamp for my feet and a light for my way.
PSALM 119:105

Now you have made yourself pure by obeying the truth.... This new life did not come from something that dies, but from something that cannot die. You were born again through God's living message that continues forever.
1 PETER 1:22–23

SEE ALSO:
Psalm 19:7

Jesus

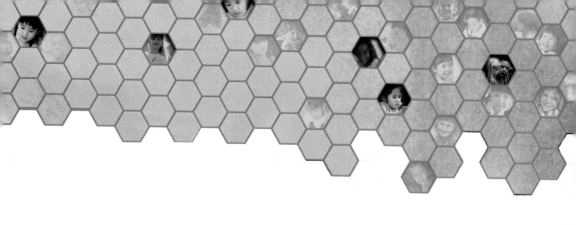

Must we obey God all the time?

Our sin is a very serious thing. Every time we do something wrong, we break God's holy law. God loves us even when we sin, but He cannot just overlook our sin. Every sin against God's law must be punished. Obeying God *most* of the time is not good enough. If you could obey God your whole life and sin against Him only one time, that one sin would be enough to make you guilty before God.

The punishment for sin against God is very severe. As God told Adam in the garden, the penalty of sin is everlasting spiritual death. There is no way we could pay for our own sins without suffering forever in hell.

Dear God:
I am sorry for my sins.

WORD SCRAMBLE

Question: When do we break God's law?

RVYEE MITE EW OD TNGIHOMES RNOGW

swer: Every time we do something wrong

Take some time to think about sin. What things have you done wrong? Ask God to forgive you.

God's Word

A person might follow all of God's law. But if he fails to obey even one command, he is guilty of breaking all the commands in that law.
JAMES 2:10

My guilt has overwhelmed me. Like a load it weighs me down.
PSALM 38:4

Everyone

sins. Not one person who has ever lived, except for Jesus, was without sin. Every time you tell a lie, or act selfishly, or talk back to your parents, you are sinning. The Good News is that when you ask God, He will forgive all your sins.

Does God want me to be punished?

God is kind, loving, and forgiving. He created us for friendship with Him. He made us to enjoy His glory. God still loves us, even though we sin against Him.

It pleases God to keep people from being punished in hell. That is why He has made a way for people to pay for their sin so they do not have to go to hell. Instead, God can take them to live with Him forever in His beautiful heaven.

We know that God cannot just overlook our sin. If He allowed us to sin and ignored it without punishing anyone, He would not really be holy. Because God *is* holy, He must require us to be holy, too.

WORD SCRAMBLE

Question: How does God feel about us, even when we sin?

ODG LILTS SOVLE SU.

PRAYER STARTER

Dear God:
Thank You for loving me, even when I sin.

Answer: God still loves us.

What do you think heaven looks like? Draw a picture of it.

WHEN YOU

do something wrong, you expect your parents to punish you, don't you? That's the way it is with God. We are all His children. And when we do things that are wrong, we can expect to be punished. But if we follow God's special plan, He will forgive us, and some day we will go to live with Him forever in heaven.

God's Word

Christ died for us while we were still sinners. In this way God shows his great love for us.
ROMANS 5:8

[God,] your eyes are too good to look at evil. You cannot stand to see people do wrong. So how can you put up with those evil people? How can you be quiet when wicked people defeat people who are better than they are?
HABAKKUK 1:13

Does God have a plan to forgive us?

Before He created the world, God planned a way to forgive sinners. He would have someone else take the punishment that sinners deserved. He would send Jesus to earth to be punished in our place.

That was God's plan even before the beginning of time. Before the world ever began, God the Father promised His Son a great gift. The Father wanted to give the Son many, many people who would love and glorify Him forever.

WORD SCRAMBLE

Question: Whom did God send to be punished in our place?

ODG NEST SUJES!

Answer: God sent Jesus!

Use the talents and abilities God gave you to thank Him for sending Jesus to earth. You can write, draw, sing—or find some other special way to say "thank You."

GOD knew Adam would sin. He knew everyone who was born after Adam would be born with a love of sin. So He planned a way to rescue people from their own sin. Do you know about Jesus? You can read about Him in your Bible in the New Testament.

God's Word

God saved us and made us his holy people. That was not because of anything we did ourselves but because of what he wanted and because of his grace. That grace was given to us through Christ Jesus before time began.
2 TIMOTHY 1:9

You were bought, but not with something that ruins like gold or silver. You were bought with the precious blood of the death of Christ, who was like a pure and perfect lamb. Christ was chosen before the world was made. But he was shown to the world in these last times for you.
1 PETER 1:18-20

SEE ALSO:
Ephesians 1:4
Isaiah 53:4-5
Titus 1:2

The story of Jesus

God sent His Son, Jesus Christ, to live on earth as a completely sinless man. Jesus was born as a baby in Bethlehem. He grew up to be a man without ever doing one wrong thing. He never had a bad attitude or an evil thought. He never said a bad word. He was God. He was perfect.

But even though He was perfect, some people did not like Him. In fact, *because* He was perfect, people who loved sin hated Him. So they killed Him by nailing Him on a cross. God allowed that to happen because on the cross, Jesus took the punishment for every person's guilt throughout history as if it were His own. By dying, He paid the penalty for our sin.

God's Word

You know that Christ came to take away sins. There is no sin in Christ.
1 JOHN 3:5

Christ suffered for you. He gave you an example to follow. So you should do as he did. "He did no sin. He never lied." [Isaiah 53:9] People insulted Christ, but he did not insult them in return. Christ suffered, but he did not threaten. He let God take care of him. God is the One who judges rightly.
1 PETER 2:21-23

Jesus was given to you, and you killed him. With the help of evil men you nailed him to a cross. But God knew all this would happen. This was God's plan which he had made long ago.
ACTS 2:23

We all have wandered away like sheep. Each of us has gone his own way. But the Lord has put on him the punishment for all the evil we have done.
ISAIAH 53:6

Christ carried our sins in his body on the cross.
1 PETER 2:24

People are made right with God by his grace, which is a free gift. They are made right with God by being made free from sin through Jesus Christ. God gave Jesus as a way to forgive sin through faith. And all of this is because of the blood of Jesus' death. This showed that God always does what is right and fair. God was right in the past when he was patient and did not punish people for their sins.
ROMANS 3:24-25

Jesus is the way our sins are taken away. And Jesus is the way that all people can have their sins taken away, too.
1 JOHN 2:2

Did Jesus want to die for our sins?

Jesus died because He chose to—because it would fulfill God's plan. Jesus knew that it would hurt to die. He did it because He loved people so much, even though they were sinners and some even hated Him.

Jesus didn't deserve to die. Wicked men beat Him, put a crown of thorns on His head, and nailed His hands and feet to the cross. They stabbed Him with a spear—all the time saying cruel things to Him.

But what hurt Jesus the most was that God, His own Father, punished Him for our sins. God did not hurt His Son to be mean. He did not do it because Jesus deserved it. He did it because there was no other way to save us from our sins. God treated His Son as if He had sinned, so that He could treat us as if we lived Jesus' perfect life.

PRAYER STARTER

Dear Jesus:
Thank You for taking the punishment for me.

WORD SCRAMBLE

Question: Why did Jesus die for us?

OT YAP HET RCIPE ROF INS

Answer: To pay the price for sin

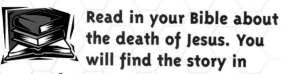

Read in your Bible about the death of Jesus. You will find the story in Matthew 27:32–61, Mark 15:21–41, Luke 23:13–49, and John 19:15–37. Think about the great gift He has given you.

WOULD YOU

let your dad punish you for the bad things someone else did? That is what Jesus did because it was the only way to pay for people's sin. That was God's plan before He created the world. Isn't that amazing? We cannot even begin to understand all it cost Jesus to become a man and die for other people's sins. The pain and sorrow He felt were worse than all the bad things that have ever happened to you and me. Yet He was willing to die like that because He loves us so much.

God's Word

Christ had no sin. But God made him become sin. God did this for us so that in Christ we could become right with God.
2 CORINTHIANS 5:21

Christ himself died for you. And that one death paid for your sins. He was not guilty, but he died for those who are guilty. He did this to bring you all to God.
1 PETER 3:18

But it was the Lord who decided to crush him and make him suffer. So the Lord made his life a penalty offering.
ISAIAH 53:10

This is how we know what real love is: Jesus gave his life for us.
1 JOHN 3:16

SEE ALSO:
Mark 8:31
Matthew 27:39-44
Mark 15:34

Is Jesus still dead?

Here's the most wonderful part of the whole story: Jesus rose from the dead! After He was killed, He was placed in a cave, and the entrance to the cave was covered with a very large slab of rock. Then, three days after he was killed, Jesus walked out alive. Some angels rolled away the rock, so that everyone could see that Jesus was gone from the grave. Many people saw Him walking around alive.

This proved that He was God and that He had defeated sin and death. After forty more days on earth, Jesus was taken up in some clouds to heaven. His followers watched Him go up. Now He is in heaven, but one day He will return to earth.

PRAYER STARTER

Dear Jesus:
I believe that You
are alive.

WORD SCRAMBLE

Question: What is the most wonderful part of the story?

SUESJ SORE MORF HET EADD.

Answer: Jesus rose from the dead.

Draw a picture of the tomb with the stone rolled away and an angel sitting on it.

Can you

imagine what it would be like today if a well-known person died and then was seen walking around? Of course, you will never see that happen. No wonder people were very surprised when Jesus rose from the grave!

God's Word

And this was the most important: that Christ died for our sins, as the Scriptures say; that he was buried and was raised to life on the third day as the Scriptures say; and that he showed himself to Peter and then to the twelve apostles. After that, Jesus showed himself to more than 500 of the believers at the same time. Most of them are still living today. But some have died. Then Jesus showed himself to James and later to all the apostles. Last of all he showed himself to me.
1 CORINTHIANS 15: 3–8

SEE ALSO:
Matthew 27
Luke 24
John 20

CHAPTER 6

Salvation

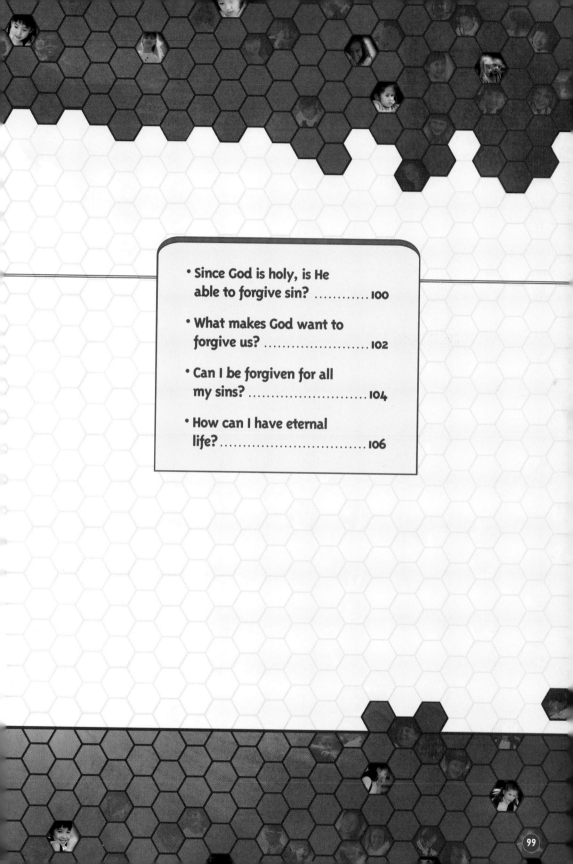

Since God is holy, is He able to forgive sin?

God is holy, and God is without sin. He has never sinned and He never will sin because God is absolutely perfect. God wants us to always obey His Word. And when we disobey Him, He promises to correct us. Even though God is sinless and even though we disobey Him, we can be sure that God loves to forgive us and that He doesn't want to punish us.

We cannot be perfectly obedient to God, no matter how hard we try. No one but God can be perfect. God knew that, and that is why He sent Jesus to be punished in our place. We must be very thankful to God for being willing to forgive us and not punish us as we deserve.

PRAYER STARTER

Thank You, God, for being willing to forgive me.

WORD SCRAMBLE

Question: Why has God never sinned?

SEUACEB EH SI SOLABTEUYL REFPECT

Answer: Because He is absolutely perfect

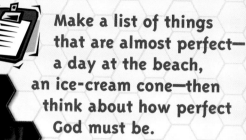

Make a list of things that are almost perfect— a day at the beach, an ice-cream cone—then think about how perfect God must be.

WHEN YOU

do something wrong, can you imagine your parents never forgiving you and punishing you for the rest of your life? Of course not! And God is like a perfect parent. He loves you more than you can ever imagine. Even though you must learn the difference between right and wrong, He will always love you and forgive you whenever you sin.

God's Word

Our guilt overwhelms us. But you forgive our sins.
PSALM 65:3

"I, I am the One who forgives all your sins. I do this to please myself. I will not remember your sins."
ISAIAH 43:25

There is no God like you. You forgive people who are guilty of sin. You don't look at the sins of your people who are left alive. You, Lord, will not stay angry forever. You enjoy being kind.
MICAH 7:18

Be kind and loving to each other. Forgive each other just as God forgave you in Christ.
EPHESIANS 4:32

What makes God want to forgive us?

God's willingness to forgive all of our sins is called grace. *Grace* is a word that means God gives us something good and precious that we don't deserve and could never earn. God loves sinners, and because of that love He wants to show them grace. He wants to give sinners what they don't deserve—a home in His heaven forever! And remember, God can do that because He punished Jesus for our sins. And Jesus was willing to take our punishment because of His love and grace.

When we ask for forgiveness, God is willing to extend His grace to us. He will forgive us. And when we die, we will live with Him forever in heaven.

WORD SCRAMBLE

Question: What does God want to give to sinners?

A EOMH NI SIH VEAHNE VEERORF

Answer: A home in His heaven forever

Forgive somebody today! Do something nice for them, or say something nice about them.

God's Word

But God's mercy is great, and he loved us very much. We were spiritually dead because of the things we did wrong against God. But God gave us new life with Christ. You have been saved by God's grace.
EPHESIANS 2:4-5

Christ died for us while we were still weak. We were living against God, but at the right time, Christ died for us. Very few people will die to save the life of someone else. Although perhaps for a good man someone might possibly die. But Christ died for us while we were still sinners. In this way God shows his great love for us.
ROMANS 5:6-8

SEE ALSO:
Ephesians 1:7
Ephesians 2:8-9

Do you

know people who are always being mean or always doing wrong things? Has someone ever hurt you so much that you found it hard to forgive? God wants us to forgive others, because that's what He does. All people have to do is ask God to forgive them, and God will give them grace.

Can I be forgiven for all my sins?

The Bible says that God can forgive any sinner who asks to be forgiven and believes in Jesus Christ. God can forgive sin and still be a holy God because Jesus was punished for our sin.

God can also treat believers as if they were perfect. That's because they get credit for every good thing Jesus ever did during His perfect life on earth. All His perfect goodness covers them like a clean, white robe.

PRAYER STARTER

Dear God:
Thank You for
forgiving me.

WORD SCRAMBLE

Question: What must we do to be forgiven?

LEEBEVI NI SUSEJ.

Answer: Believe in Jesus.

What have you learned about Jesus? Share what you've learned with at least one friend.

God's Word

Wash away all my guilt and make me clean again.
PSALM 51:2

The Lord has covered me with clothes of salvation. He has covered me with a coat of goodness. I am like a bridegroom dressed for his wedding. I am like a bride dressed in jewels.
ISAIAH 61:10

Now that I belong to Christ, I am right with God and this being right does not come from my following the law. It comes from God through faith.
PHILIPPIANS 3:9

YOUR MOTHER

cannot forgive you for your sin. Your father can't. Neither can your pastor or your friends or anyone else on earth. God is the only One who can forgive you. You can have your sins forgiven if you trust Jesus and ask Him to forgive you. Wouldn't you like to know that someday you will go to live with Him in heaven forever?

How can I have eternal life?

God wants to forgive you for your sin. He loves you so much that He sent Jesus to earth to die in your place. God has promised to give eternal life to everyone who trusts Him for forgiveness. If you are sorry for your sin, willing to turn away from it, and believe in Jesus as your Lord and Savior, He promises to give *you* eternal life, too.

WORD SCRAMBLE

Question: If we trust God for forgiveness, what will we receive?

LANTERE EIFL

Answer: Eternal life

Did you ask God to be your Savior? If you did, this is a very special day for you. Tell someone about it!

You can be forgiven by praying to God right now and asking Him to be your Savior. Would you like to do that? God *promised* never to say no to anyone who really trusts Him. So if you truly believe in Him with all your heart, you can be sure He has given you eternal life.

God's Word

"For God loved the world so much that he gave his only Son. God gave his Son so that whoever believes in him may not be lost, but have eternal life."
JOHN 3:16

"I tell you the truth. Whoever hears what I say and believes in the One who sent me has eternal life. He will not be judged guilty. He has already left death and has entered into life."
JOHN 5:24

But some people did accept him. They believed in him.
JOHN 1:12

"Everyone who sees the Son and believes in him has eternal life. I will raise him up on the last day. This is what my Father wants."
JOHN 6:40

SEE ALSO:
John 7:37–38
John 11:26

CHAPTER 7

Worship

Why should we thank God?

When someone shows love for us by giving us gifts, we should be thankful. Being thankful is as wonderful and as important as giving.

Since everything good is a gift from the Lord, He deserves our thanks. He gave us our lives, our parents, our friends, and our homes. His gifts to us never stop. God gives us food, clothing, and all kinds of good things. Best of all, He gives us forgiveness for all our sins and promises us eternal life through His Son.

WORD SCRAMBLE

Question: What does God deserve?

SENDLES ASNKHT

nswer: Endless thanks

PRAYER STARTER

Dear God:
Thank You for Your
abundant gifts.

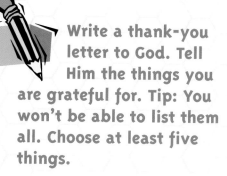

Write a thank-you letter to God. Tell Him the things you are grateful for. Tip: You won't be able to list them all. Choose at least five things.

God's Word

GOD deserves endless thanks. Just think of all that He has given you. When you go to bed at night, you have a warm bed to sleep in. Some of you have pets that you love. I'm sure there are things that you like to do. Are you good at schoolwork, sports, art, or music? Everything you have and everything you are is because of God. Take time today to thank Him for all that He has given you.

The story of Jesus and ten sick men

There is a wonderful story in the Bible about being thankful.

There were ten men who were very sick. Jesus was walking through a small town when He met those ten men. They saw Jesus, but they would not come close to Him because they had such an awful disease. They knew Jesus could heal them, so they asked Him to make them well. Jesus was kind. He did what they asked, and by His great power, He made all ten of them completely well.

But only one of the men came back to say thank you to Jesus. He praised God. He bowed down to worship, and he thanked Jesus.

To be so sick that you might die, and to have the Lord heal you of that sickness should cause anyone to thank Him. But nine men did not. They didn't thank God or worship Him. They were not real believers in Jesus. They wanted Him to heal them, but they did not really love Him. Ten men were healed from their disease. But the man who really loved Jesus was the only one healed from his sin.

We should all be like the man who gave thanks. He worshiped Jesus. That was the proof that he *really* believed. Giving thanks and worshiping God are the most normal things in the world for people who really trust the Lord.

God's Word

Jesus was on his way to Jerusalem. Traveling from Galilee to Samaria, he came into a small town. Ten men met him there. These men did not come close to Jesus, because they all had a harmful skin disease. But they called to him, "Jesus! Master! Please help us!"

When Jesus saw the men, he said, "Go and show yourselves to the priests." While the ten men were going, they were healed. When one of them saw that he was healed, he went back to Jesus. He praised God in a loud voice. Then he bowed down at Jesus' feet and thanked him. (This man was a Samaritan.)

Jesus asked, "Ten men were healed; where are the other nine? Is this Samaritan the only one who came back to thank God?" Then Jesus said to him, "Stand up and go on your way. You were healed because you believed."

LUKE 17:11–19

We worship God through his Spirit. We are proud to be in Christ Jesus. And we do not trust in ourselves or anything we can do.

PHILIPPIANS 3:3

How should we worship God?

God wants us to worship Him and Him only. Remember—that is one of the main reasons He created us.

How do we worship God? We worship Him by giving thanks for everything He has done for us. We worship by singing praise to Him. We worship when we pray to Him and tell Him how great He is. And we worship when we go to church and gather with other believers to sing and pray and listen to preaching about the Bible.

WORD SCRAMBLE

Question: What is one of the main reasons God created us?

OT ROSHWIP IMH

Answer: To worship Him

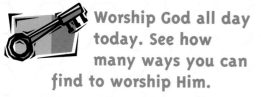

Worship God all day today. See how many ways you can find to worship Him.

Do you

know you can worship God in everything you do? Everything you do (except when you sin) can be done to glorify God. And since God is a Spirit and He is everywhere, you can worship Him anywhere. No matter what you are doing—playing sports, drawing, singing, studying— do your very best, and you will glorify God.

God's Word

It is good to praise the Lord, to sing praises to God Most High.
PSALM 92:1

Come into his city with songs of thanksgiving. Come into his courtyards with songs of praise. Thank him, and praise his name.
PSALM 100:4

So if you eat, or if you drink, or if you do anything, do everything for the glory of God.
1 CORINTHIANS 10:31

Everything you say and everything you do should all be done for Jesus your Lord. And in all you do, give thanks to God the Father through Jesus.
COLOSSIANS 3:17

SEE ALSO:
Exodus 20:3
1 Thessalonians 5:17
Matthew 6:9-10
John 4:21, 23-24

Does God see everything we do?

God sees everything you do. He even knows your thoughts. And if you always remember that, everything you do can be done as worship to God. If you always remember that God is watching you, it will help you want to do good things. And when God sees and approves of what you are doing, you glorify Him. If He is pleased with how you act, what you say, and what you think about, you are giving Him glory. That is a kind of worship.

WORD SCRAMBLE

Question: What will help us remember to do good things?

ODG SI HATCWING.

PRAYER STARTER

Dear God:
Help me to glorify You
in everything I do.

Spend today remembering that God is watching you. See if it doesn't make a difference in the way you act.

WHEN YOU

do something wrong, God sees. He sees when you disobey your parents. He sees when you fight with your brother, sister, or friends. He sees when you lie or when you take something that doesn't belong to you. God sees *everything*. Remembering that will help you to do things that are right and good.

God's Word

Lord, you have examined me. You know all about me. You know when I sit down and when I get up. You know my thoughts before I think them. You know where I go and where I lie down. You know well everything I do. Lord, even before I say a word, you already know what I am going to say. You are all around me—in front and in back. You have put your hand on me. Your knowledge is amazing to me. It is more than I can understand.

PSALM 139:1-6

Will we worship God in heaven?

In heaven, the worship of God never stops. People in heaven think about God all the time. They always thank Him and praise Him for how wonderful He is. Someday, we will live in heaven, worshiping God forever.

Right here on earth we should begin to worship God the way we will worship Him in heaven. We can start doing that by keeping Him in our thoughts all the time.

PRAYER STARTER

Dear God:
I think of You all day long.

WORD SCRAMBLE

Question: What will we do in heaven?

EW ILLW ROWHIPS ODG.

Answer: We will worship God.

Make a list of things that will help you to think of God all day long.

God's Word

And [the people in heaven] are before the throne of God. They worship God day and night in his temple.
REVELATION 7:15

Day and night they never stop saying: "Holy, holy, holy is the Lord God All-Powerful. He was, he is, and he is coming."
REVELATION 4:8

How can you keep God in your thoughts? You can think about things that are good and be grateful to Him for them. Thanking God for good things is one way to worship Him. That is why God commands us to think about things that are good, true, right, and pure. Every time you thank God for these things, you are worshiping Him.

Is worship really important?

We can't really worship God unless He is the most important Person in our lives. If anyone or anything else is more important to us than God, then that is the real god we worship. Anything or anyone we love more than God is an idol, or a false god to us.

Real worship starts with loving God more than anything or anyone else in the whole world. When we always remember that God is the most important Person in our lives, everything we do can bring Him glory. And when we remember to thank Him, obey Him, and love Him more than anything else, that is the best kind of worship.

PRAYER STARTER
Dear God:
I want to put You
first in my life.

WORD SCRAMBLE

Question: What are false gods called?

SALFE DOGS REA DELALC SOLID.

Answer: False gods are called idols.

Read a story about idols in your Bible. Read Acts 17:16-34. It is the story of Paul, a man who loved God and worshiped Him. It tells what Paul said to the people of Greece when he found them worshiping idols.

Do you

like soccer or gymnastics? Those are good things that can be done to glorify God. But those things—or anything else you love— can become idols. If you have an idol, you cannot really worship God, even if you pretend to worship. Your friends can become idols too, if you let them be more important to you than God is. Television can become an idol. Music, school, hobbies— *anything*—can become more important to you than God. And any kind of idol will keep you from worshiping God in the way that you should.

God's Word

Love the Lord your God with all your heart, soul and strength.
DEUTERONOMY 6:5

The Lord is great; he should be praised. He should be honored more than all the gods. All the gods of the nations are only idols. But the Lord made the skies.
1 CHRONICLES 16:25-26

So, dear children, keep yourselves away from false gods.
1 JOHN 5:21

"'Love the Lord your God with all your heart, soul and mind.' This is the first and most important command."
MATTHEW 22:37-38

Prayer

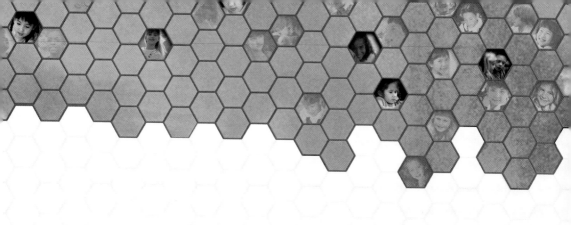

What is prayer?

Talking to God is called *prayer.* You can talk to the Lord anywhere you are, at any time, because He is always with you.

The Bible says that God wants us to pray to Him all the time. That doesn't mean we can never talk to anyone else. But it means we should never stop talking to God.

The wonderful thing about talking to God is that He is better than any other friend we can talk to. He cares about us more than anyone else. He has the power to give us everything we need. God *wants* us to ask Him for whatever we need. And He loves to answer our prayers by giving us what we ask for.

PRAYER STARTER

Dear God:
Thank You for never being too busy to listen.

WORD SCRAMBLE

Question: What is talking to God called?

LIKATNG OT ODG SI LEDLAC EARPRY.

Answer: Talking to God is called prayer.

Find a quiet place where you can be alone with God. Spend some time talking to Him. You can tell Him whatever is on your mind.

Have you

ever wanted to talk to someone about a problem, but they were too busy? That will never happen when you talk to God. The Lord will be there for you any time you want to talk to Him—no matter what time of day or night. Isn't that wonderful?

God's Word

Never stop praying.
1 THESSALONIANS 5:17

Pray in the Spirit at all times. Pray with all kinds of prayers, and ask for everything you need. To do this you must always be ready. Never give up. Always pray for all God's people.
EPHESIANS 6:18

So I tell you, continue to ask, and God will give to you. Continue to search, and you will find. Continue to knock, and the door will open for you. Yes, if a person continues asking, he will receive. If he continues searching, he will find. And if he continues knocking, the door will open for him.
LUKE 11:9–10

Does God always know what we're thinking?

God knows exactly what you're thinking all the time. You do not have to speak out loud to talk to Him. You can pray to Him in your mind, and He hears your prayer. That means you can pray no matter where you are and no matter what is going on around you.

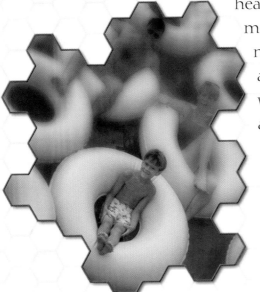

WORD SCRAMBLE

Question: Where should I go to pray?

ODG SERAH OUY WEVERHERE UOY REA.

Answer: God hears you wherever you are.

Spend today praying to God in your mind. He will be with you wherever you go, whether you are with others or by yourself.

How many times have you been in a tough situation and not known what to do? Do you know that God was there with you? God always knows just what you are thinking, and He always hears your prayers.

God's Word

While Hannah kept praying, Eli watched her mouth. She was praying in her heart. Her lips moved, but her voice was not heard.
1 SAMUEL 1:12–13

"When you pray, don't be like the hypocrites. They love to stand in the synagogues and on the street corners and pray loudly. They want people to see them pray. I tell you the truth. They already have their full reward. When you pray, you should go into your room and close the door. Then pray to your Father who cannot be seen. Your Father can see what is done in secret, and he will reward you."
MATTHEW 6:5–6

SEE ALSO:
Psalm 62:8
Jeremiah 29:13

Does God always give us what we want?

God doesn't always give us everything we ask for. Sometimes God says no to us because He loves us. God will give us only what is good for us. He will not give us things that would be bad for us or would hurt us.

When we pray, we should ask for things that help us to be more like God wants us to be.

For example: if you ask God for wisdom, He will give it to you. But if you ask God for something selfish, He will probably say no.

WORD SCRAMBLE

Question: Why does God sometimes say no?

CABESUE ODG VESLO SU

Answer: Because God loves us

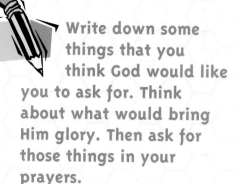

Write down some things that you think God would like you to ask for. Think about what would bring Him glory. Then ask for those things in your prayers.

Sometimes

when you ask your parents for something you really want, they say no. Even if you keep asking, they still say no. They know better than you do what is good for you. When your parents say no, it is not because they don't love you. It is because they know what you want is not good for you. When they say no, it is because they want you to have only what is good. And that's the way it is with God, too. He will always do what is best for you.

God's Word

If any of you needs wisdom, you should ask God for it. God is generous. He enjoys giving to all people, so God will give you wisdom.
JAMES 1:5

Do you think the Scripture means nothing? It says, "The Spirit that God made to live in us wants us for himself alone."
JAMES 4:5

The thing you should want most is God's kingdom and doing what God wants. Then all these other things you need will be given to you.
MATTHEW 6:33

Does God know exactly what we need?

God is even wiser than our parents, and He knows *exactly* what is best for us. When we ask God for things, we must trust Him to know what is best.

Sometimes we ask for things that are selfish or for things that might become idols to us. We ask for things we don't really need. We might even ask for things that would be bad for us. When we ask for things like that, God will not give us what we ask for.

If we ask for something God wants us to ask for, something we need or something that glorifies Him, He will give it to us. God loves to say yes to the prayers of those who love Him.

PRAYER STARTER

Dear God:
Thank You for giving me just what I need.

WORD SCRAMBLE

Question: When we ask God for things, what must we do?

EW STUM STRUT ODG OT OD THWA SI STEB.

Answer: We must trust God to do what is best.

Make a poster for your room with these words: GOD KNOWS BEST.

God's Word

"And if you ask for anything in my name, I will do it for you. Then the Father's glory will be shown through the Son. If you ask me for anything in my name, I will do it."
JOHN 14:13-14

And God gives us the things we ask for. We receive these things because we obey God's commands, and we do what pleases him.
1 JOHN 3:22

"Remain in me and follow my teachings. If you do this, then you can ask for anything you want, and it will be given to you."
JOHN 15:7

SEE ALSO:
James 4:3
John 16:23
Proverbs 15:29

Do you know what happens when God answers your prayers? He shows you His power and His glory. It also makes your faith stronger to know that God has answered your prayers. He is pleased whenever you pray, and He loves to answer you.

Why doesn't God answer my prayers right away?

Sometimes God wants us to keep praying for something, so He does not answer quickly. Jesus told a story about a woman who kept going to a judge to ask him to punish her enemy. At first, the judge didn't answer the woman. Finally, after a long time, he gave her what she asked for, just because she kept asking.

God wants us to keep asking for what we need. Sometimes He waits before answering, but it is not because He doesn't care. He always knows the best time to answer our prayers. Often the best time is not as soon as we think. God wants us to be patient and keep praying.

WORD SCRAMBLE

Question: When God doesn't answer right away, what should we do?

EB TENTPIA DAN PEKE GRAYPIN.

Answer: Be patient and keep praying.

PRAYER STARTER
Dear God:
Thank You for knowing when to answer my prayers.

Write a story about being patient. In your story tell why it was worth it to wait.

It's Hard

to be patient, isn't it? It's like waiting to open your presents on Christmas morning. You know that something good is going to happen, but you have to wait. It is like that with God sometimes. If what we are praying for is right and good, we know we will receive it. But sometimes we must wait because only God knows the best time to answer our prayers.

God's Word

We can come to God with no doubts. This means that when we ask God for things (and those things agree with what God wants for us), then God cares about what we say. God listens to us every time we ask him. So we know that he gives us the things that we ask from him.

1 JOHN 5:14–15

Enjoy serving the Lord. And he will give you what you want.

PSALM 37:4

Should I believe that God will answer my prayers?

God wants us to *believe* that He will answer our prayers. If we don't really believe He will answer us, then He won't. That is because prayer is a way of showing God that we believe in Him. And He will reward us if we believe. When we don't have faith in God, then our prayers don't glorify Him. And praying without believing is an insult to God.

WORD SCRAMBLE

Question: What does God want us to believe about prayer?

HTAT EH ILWL NASERW RUO RYAPRSE

PRAYER STARTER

Dear God:
I believe that You will answer my prayers.

Think about what it means to believe. Can you write a poem about it?

Another

thing that is hard is believing without seeing. You expect to see something change when you pray, and when it doesn't you might lose faith. It is very important to trust that God is there and that He hears you. It is also very important to believe that He *will* answer your prayers. God isn't like your friends or other people who might let you down. God will never let you down. He will always do what is best for you. That's why sometimes He says "yes," sometimes "no," and sometimes "wait."

God's Word

"If you believe, you will get anything you ask for in prayer."
MATTHEW 21:22

"So I tell you to ask for things in prayer. And if you believe that you have received those things, then they will be yours."
MARK 11:24

When you ask God, you must believe. Do not doubt God. Anyone who doubts is like a wave in the sea. The wind blows the wave up and down. He who doubts is thinking two different things at the same time. He cannot decide about anything he does. A person like that should not think that he will receive anything from the Lord.
JAMES 1:6-8

Is there a special way to pray?

Our prayers don't have to be long. And we don't have to talk to God with special words. Praying to God is very much like talking to anyone else, except that we can't see God, and we can't hear His voice talking back to us. But we know that God is there, and we know that He hears us. Most of your praying will be private—between you and God alone.

WORD SCRAMBLE

Question: Where will most of your praying be done?

NI RATEVIP—NEETWEB ODG DNA LYMFES

Answer: In private—between God and myself

Read Jesus' prayer in your Bible. You will find it in Matthew 6:9-13.

WHEN YOU

go to school, a teacher is there to teach you new things. God sent a special Teacher to earth. It was His Son, Jesus. Jesus taught His followers how to pray. The example He gave them was very short and very simple. It was a perfect prayer.

God's Word

"When you pray, you should go into your room and close the door. Then pray to your Father who cannot be seen. Your Father can see what is done in secret, and he will reward you. And when you pray, don't be like those people who don't know God. They continue saying things that mean nothing. They think that God will hear them because of the many things they say. Don't be like them. Your Father knows the things you need before you ask him."

MATTHEW 6:6-8

SEE ALSO:
Matthew 6:9-13

How should we pray?

This is how Jesus taught His followers to pray:

1. **Praise God. Tell Him how wonderful He is.**

2. **Pray that He will do whatever *He* wants, even if it is not what *we* want.**

3. Tell God that we trust Him to do what is best, no matter how He answers our prayers.

4. **Pray for what we know we need. That includes praying for what other people need—especially our friends and family.**

5. **Ask God's forgiveness for the things we have done wrong. At the same time, forgive others who have done wrong things to us.**

6. **Ask God to help us not to do wrong things.**

If you pray for the right things, and you really love and trust God, He promises to hear and answer.

And when He answers, your faith in Him will grow strong.

PRAYER STARTER

Dear God:
Thank You for answering my prayers.

WORD SCRAMBLE

Question: What should you tell God no matter how He answers your prayers?

I RTSUT OUY OT OD HWAT SI ESBT.

Answer: I trust you to do what is best.

Find a private place where you can be alone with God. Tell Him what you have learned about prayer.

Have you

discovered that prayer is a wonderful thing? The more you pray, the closer you feel to God. If you are in a new place, and you feel all alone, God is there to talk to. When you are afraid, and you don't want your friends to know it, you can pray to God in your mind. He is always with you. God always hears you, no matter where you are.

God's Word

[Jesus] kneeled down and prayed, . . . "Do what you want, not what I want."
LUKE 22:41–42

"'Give us the food we need for each day.'"
LUKE 11:3

"'Forgive us the sins we have done, because we forgive every person who has done wrong to us.'"
LUKE 11:4

"When you are praying, and you remember that you are angry with another person about something, then forgive him. If you do this, then your Father in heaven will also forgive your sins."
MARK 11:25

When a good man prays, great things happen.
JAMES 5:16

Church

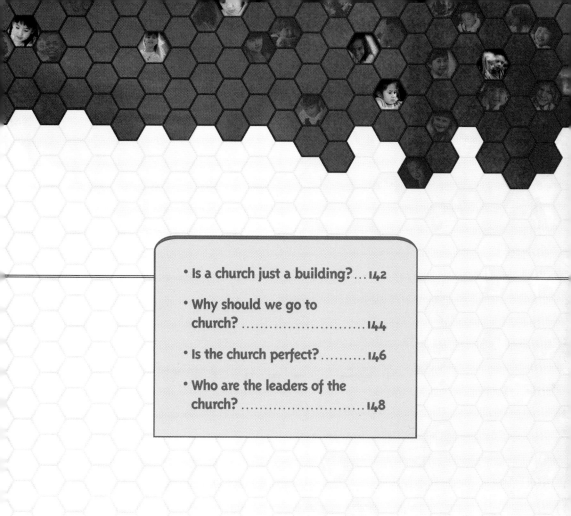

Is a church just a building?

When you think of a church, you probably think of the building where you go with your family to worship God. But the church is more than a building. In fact, you could take away the building and you would still have a church. The *real* church is not the building. It is the people.

When Jesus said, "I will build my church," He wasn't talking about a building. He was talking about people. In fact, He was talking about *all* the people who would ever be saved from their sins— everyone who truly believes in Him. All those people together make up the church.

WORD SCRAMBLE

Question: What is the church?

LLA HET POPLEE HOW RTLYU LEEBEVI NI EUSSJ

Answer: All the people who truly believe in Jesus

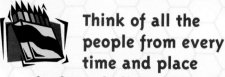

Think of all the people from every time and place who have believed in Jesus. Draw a picture to show some of God's people from other parts of the world.

WHEN you go to church on Sundays, the church you go to is just a very small part of the whole church. The church is everyone from every time and place who has truly believed in Jesus. The church includes everyone who ever *will* truly believe in Jesus, too. One day, the whole church will be together forever in heaven with Jesus. But for now, the church meets all over the world in different places. The church is a very, very large group of people—more people than you could ever count.

God's Word

"I will build my church on this rock. The power of death will not be able to defeat my church."
MATTHEW 16:18

To the church of God in Corinth, to those people who have been made holy in Christ Jesus. You were called to be God's holy people with all people everywhere who trust in the name of the Lord Jesus Christ—their Lord and ours.
1 CORINTHIANS 1:2

I looked, and there was a great number of people. There were so many people that no one could count them. They were from every nation, tribe, people, and language of the earth. They were all standing before the throne and before the Lamb. They wore white robes and had palm branches in their hands. They were shouting in a loud voice, "Salvation belongs to our God, who sits on the throne, and to the Lamb."
REVELATION 7:9-10

Why should we go to church?

We all need each other. The Bible compares the whole church to a body. Your body is made up of many parts. Some of those parts are fingers, eyes, ears, a head, and feet. All of the parts of your body must work together. The parts all work together to make you what you are. Each part has its own job to do, and all of the parts are important.

That's how the church is. All believers have something they can do well. God has given us all gifts that we can use for the good of everyone else. Some people sing, preach, or teach. Some people are good at helping people who hurt. Others are good at helping people who have special needs. Everyone is good at *something*. Every believer should do whatever he or she is good at to help the whole church.

PRAYER STARTER

Dear God:
I want to use my special gifts to help the church.

WORD SCRAMBLE

Question: What is the church like?

HET CRUHCH SI KILE A DOBY.

Answer: The church is like a body.

Do something today that will help someone else. Try to do something good for someone every day!

WHEN you hurt your toe, you feel the pain all over your body, don't you? That's how it is with the church. When one member is hurting, everyone feels the pain. When one believer is sad, others share the sadness. Doesn't it make us feel better when other people share our pain and sadness? People in the church never have to be all alone. They always have other people who can help them and encourage them when they feel bad. Everyone in the church gives strength to everyone else.

God's Word

If one part of the body suffers, then all the other parts suffer with it. Or if one part of our body is honored, then all the other parts share its honor. All of you together are the body of Christ. Each one of you is a part of that body.
1 CORINTHIANS 12:26-27

There are different kinds of gifts; but they are all from the same Spirit. There are different ways to serve; but all these ways are from the same Lord. And there are different ways that God works in people; but all these ways are from the same God. God works in us all in everything we do. Something from the Spirit can be seen in each person, to help everyone.
1 CORINTHIANS 12:4-7

SEE ALSO:
1 Corinthians 12:13-19
1 Corinthians 12:25
1 Corinthians 12:20-24
Romans 15:1-2

Is the church perfect?

No church on earth is perfect. The church is made up of people, so it is not perfect. In heaven, the church will be completely perfect.

Not everyone who goes to church really loves God. Some people who go to church don't obey the Bible the way they should. Sometimes a whole church will stop believing and teaching the Bible. When that happens, the church is no longer a real church—even though people still call it a church.

Even though the real church is not perfect yet, it is the closest thing to heaven on earth. The church is where God's people gather to worship Him. By sharing our gifts with other believers as we worship, we help each other become stronger.

WORD SCRAMBLE

Question: What should be taught and believed in church?

HET ILEBB

Answer: The Bible

PRAYER STARTER

Dear God:
I believe in what
the Bible says.

Invite a friend to go with you to church.

Do you go to Sunday school?

Do you attend church? Sunday school and church are good places to meet new friends who are believers in Christ. You need to be part of a church where the Bible is believed and taught and where people really love God and want to obey Him. You should never stop going to church. You need to be with other believers, and they need to be with you.

God's Word

So, brothers, what should you do? When you meet together, one person has a song. Another has a teaching. Another has a new truth from God. Another speaks in a different language, and another person interprets that language. The purpose of all these things should be to help the church grow strong.
1 CORINTHIANS 14:26

You should not stay away from the church meetings, as some are doing. But you should meet together and encourage each other.
HEBREWS 10:25

Who are the leaders of the church?

God has given special leaders to the church to teach us and help us with our problems. That's why churches have pastors and teachers. The Bible tells us we should listen to their teaching and obey what they teach us from God's Word. God has placed them there for our good, and we should show them respect and try to make their job a joy for them.

PRAYER STARTER

Dear God:
Thank You for my pastor and the other church leaders.

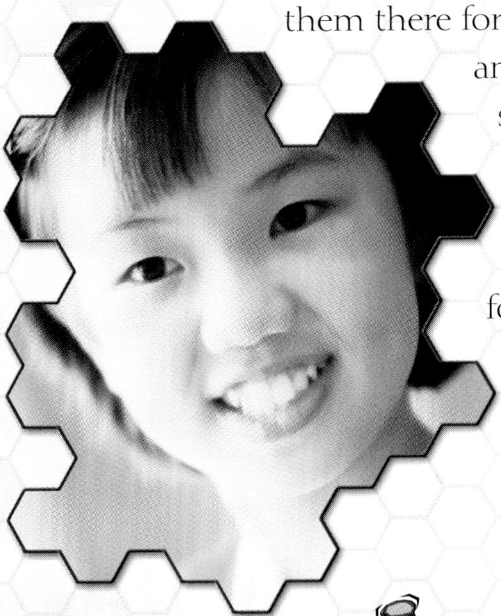

WORD SCRAMBLE

Question: Who is the head of the church?

SUSEJ RSTCHI

nswer: Jesus Christ

Make a list of reasons why the church is very important.

Just as your body has a head with a brain that does all of its thinking, the church also has a head. The Head of the church is Jesus Christ. He is the leader of the whole church, and He loves the church like a husband should love his wife. So the church is very, very important to Jesus. And that is why the church should be important to us, too.

God's Word

And Christ gave gifts to men—he made some to be apostles, some to be prophets, some to go and tell the Good News, and some to have the work of caring for and teaching God's people. Christ gave those gifts to prepare God's holy people for the work of serving. He gave those gifts to make the body of Christ stronger.
EPHESIANS 4:11–12

Obey your leaders and be under their authority. These men are watching you because they are responsible for your souls. Obey them so that they will do this work with joy, not sadness. It will not help you to make their work hard.
HEBREWS 13:17

The husband is the head of the wife, as Christ is the head of the church. The church is Christ's body—Christ is the Savior of the body.
EPHESIANS 5:23

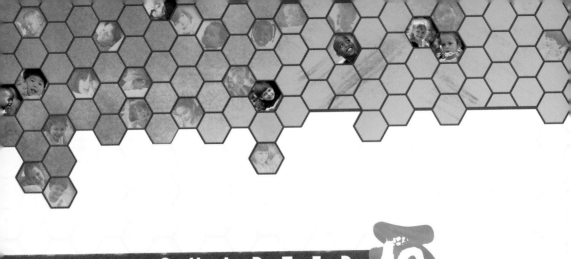

Forgiveness

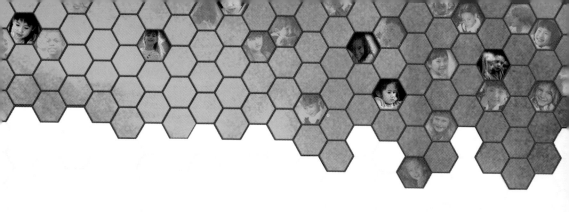

Why should we forgive one another?

God is glad to forgive the bad things we do because He is so loving and kind. But God only forgives people who are truly sorry for their sin and who ask Him for forgiveness.

Forgiveness is not only about God forgiving us. It is also about us forgiving others. God wants us to

forgive others, too. When we forgive people who have done bad things to us, we do what God would do—we show His love to others.

WORD SCRAMBLE

Question: Why should we forgive other people?

OT OWHS ODSG VOEL OT HETM

Answer: To show God's love to them

What does it mean to forgive someone? Write a story or poem about it.

Do you

get angry when your friends do bad things to you, or when they say unkind things about you? Of course you do. But it is wrong to hold that anger in your heart. God commands us to forgive others because He has forgiven us so much.

God's Word

Be kind and loving to each other. Forgive each other just as God forgave you in Christ.
EPHESIANS 4:32

You are God's children whom he loves. So try to be like God. Live a life of love. Love other people just as Christ loved us. Christ gave himself for us—he was a sweet-smelling offering and sacrifice to God.
EPHESIANS 5:1–2

"'The Lord doesn't become angry quickly. The Lord has great love. The Lord forgives sin and law breaking. He has great mercy. But the Lord does not forget to punish guilty people.'"
NUMBERS 14:18

SEE ALSO:
Joel 2:13

The story of Jesus and the man who would not forgive

Jesus told a story about a man who accepted forgiveness for himself but would not forgive someone else.

The man was a servant who owed a huge amount of money to a king—far more money than he could ever pay back. When he couldn't pay the money he owed, the king wanted to get some of his money back by selling everything the man had, including his family.

The man fell on his knees, and he begged the king to forgive him. The king felt so sorry for the man that he forgave everything he owed. He erased his debt entirely.

Of course the man was very happy. But then he remembered that another man owed him some money. It was a very small amount of money, but too much for the other man to pay back right away because he was very poor. So he begged the first man to forgive him.

Even though that first man had been forgiven for so much, he refused to forgive the other man for such a small amount. He had him locked in a special prison where people worked for many years to pay off their debts.

Many people knew that the king had forgiven the first man for such a large amount. And, of course, they were upset about what he did to the second man. So they told the king what happened. The king became so angry with the first man that he punished him by throwing him in prison, too.

Jesus used that story as a lesson about forgiveness. He said if we refuse to forgive one another, God will be angry with us in the same way that the king was angry with the unforgiving servant.

God's Word

Be kind and loving to each other. Forgive each other just as God forgave you in Christ.
EPHESIANS 4:32

Do not be angry with each other, but forgive each other. If someone does wrong to you, then forgive him. Forgive each other because the Lord forgave you.
COLOSSIANS 3:13

"If your brother sins against you seven times in one day, but he says that he is sorry each time, then forgive him."
LUKE 17:4

Whom does God want us to forgive?

God wants us to forgive even our worst enemies because that is what God does when He forgives those who have disobeyed and dishonored Him.

God has forgiven us so much that we must never refuse to forgive others. Our sin against God is a far, far greater evil than any wrong others might do to us. If we refuse to forgive, it is like thinking we are better than God.

PRAYER STARTER

Dear God:
Help me to forgive those who sin against me.

WORD SCRAMBLE

Question: Whom does God want us to forgive?

ODG STAWN SU OT VIGEROF DRYBOYEVE.

Answer: God wants us to forgive everybody.

Is there someone you
need to forgive?
Find a way to do it
today. You will feel much
better after you forgive.

God's Word

"I say to you who are
listening to me, love your
enemies. Do good to
those who hate you.
Ask God to bless those
who say bad things to
you. Pray for those who
are cruel to you. If anyone
slaps you on one cheek,
let him slap the other
cheek too. If someone
takes your coat, do not
stop him from taking your
shirt. Give to everyone
who asks you. When a
person takes something
that is yours, don't ask for
it back. Do for other
people what you want
them to do for you."
LUKE 6:27–31

"Yes, if you forgive others
for the things they do
wrong, then your Father in
heaven will also forgive
you for the things you do
wrong. But if you don't
forgive the wrongs of
others, then your Father in
heaven will not forgive
the wrong things you do."
MATTHEW 6:14–15

IS there someone who
is always mean to
you? Or maybe you
have a friend who lets you down
again and again. Sometimes it is
not easy to forgive. When someone hurts you or sins against
you over and over, you might
be tempted to hang on to your
anger and refuse to forgive. But
that is *always* the wrong thing
to do. Being unforgiving can
keep you from enjoying God's
forgiveness.

The story of Joseph and his brothers

God is able to make good things happen, even through the bad things other people do to us. The story of Joseph, in the Old Testament, is a good example.

Joseph's brothers did a mean thing to him. They threw him in a well. They were going to let him die in there, but they decided to sell him as a slave instead. So Joseph was taken to Egypt. It was a place far away from his home and his parents. Joseph's brothers deceived their father about what had happened to Joseph. They made their father believe that a wild animal had killed him.

In Egypt, God blessed Joseph. He used him to save the whole country during a time when food was very hard to find.

One day, Joseph's brothers came to Egypt looking for food. By then, Joseph was one of the most powerful men in Egypt. He had become so important that he was the person his brothers had to go to for help. Many years had passed, so his brothers did not even recognize him. But Joseph knew who they were, and in his heart he had already forgiven them for what they had done to him.

Joseph told his brothers not to feel guilty for the way they treated him because it had been God's will. He then sent for his entire family to come live with him in Egypt, where he took care of them during the food shortage. Because Joseph was willing to forgive his brothers, he was able to have this happy reunion with his family.

We know that in everything God works for the good of those who love him.
ROMANS 8:28

When the Midianite traders came by, the brothers took Joseph out of the well. They sold him to the Ishmaelites for eight ounces of silver. And the Ishmaelites took him to Egypt.
GENESIS 37:28

The brothers killed a goat and dipped Joseph's long-sleeved robe in its blood. Then they brought the robe to their father. They said, "We found this robe. Look it over carefully. See if it is your son's robe." Jacob looked it over and said, "It is my son's robe! Some savage animal has eaten him. My son Joseph has been torn to pieces!"
GENESIS 37:31-33

Why did Joseph forgive his brothers?

Were you surprised that Joseph forgave his brothers so easily? After all, he had suffered a lot because of what they did to him. He was separated from his home and his parents for many years. He even spent time in prison in Egypt. And yet he forgave his brothers for everything they did to him.

Joseph knew that God was still in control of his life. He believed that God had a good purpose for allowing him to be sent to Egypt and even to prison. Joseph trusted God to be good to him even when his own brothers treated him badly. He paid more attention to the good things God did for him than he did to the bad things his brothers did to him. And that's why Joseph forgave them.

WORD SCRAMBLE

Question: When are we most like God?

NEWH EW VROFEIG

Answer: When we forgive

In one day, Joseph went from being a prisoner to being a Ruler over Egypt. Read about it in your Bible. You will find the story in Genesis 41.

God's Word

"Don't be angry with yourselves because you sold me here. God sent me here ahead of you to save people's lives."
GENESIS 45:5

"You meant to hurt me. But God turned your evil into good. It was to save the lives of many people. And it is being done. So don't be afraid."
GENESIS 50:20-21

It's sometimes hard to forgive, isn't it? Sometimes we have to forgive people, even when they are not sorry. Have you ever had to do that? If you did, maybe that person kept on sinning against you. And that hurt, didn't it? But remember—we are never more like God than when we forgive someone. If you want to show people God's love and goodness, fill your heart with forgiveness for others.

CHAPTER **11**

Evangelism

Why should we tell others about Jesus?

When you have good news, you want to share it with other people. And you know some *very* good news. It is the Good News about God's forgiveness of sin. It is the best news ever! That is why you'll want to tell others about it.

Jesus commanded His followers to take the Good News into all the world. He said we should tell as many people as possible about Him because He is the only one who can save people from their sins.

PRAYER STARTER
Dear God:
I want to know how to spread the Good News.

WORD SCRAMBLE

Question: What is the Good News about?

SOGD RINGSOFEVES FO ISN

Answer: God's forgiveness of sin

Make a list of your friends who do not know Jesus.

God's Word

Jesus said to the followers, "Go everywhere in the world. Tell the Good News to everyone."
MARK 16:15

"Jesus is the only One who can save people. His name is the only power in the world that has been given to save people. And we must be saved through him!"
ACTS 4:12

WHEN YOU

get a new pet or a new bicycle or a special toy, you hurry to tell your friends, don't you? We all love to share good news. And Jesus Christ is the best news of all. All of your friends need to know about Jesus. If they do not know about how He can forgive their sin, be sure to tell them. It is very important that they know.

What does it mean to be a witness?

The Bible says that when we tell people about Christ, we are *witnesses*. Witnesses are people in a courtroom who tell about what they have seen and heard. As witnesses for Jesus, we tell people about what He has done and said.

It is important to live in a way that honors Christ if we are going to tell other people about Him. People who disobey Christ are not good witnesses. It does no good to tell people that Jesus is wonderful if you act as if you don't really care about Him. We witness by our behavior—not just by our words.

PRAYER STARTER

Dear God:
Help me to behave in a way that honors You.

WORD SCRAMBLE

Question: Besides words, how else do we witness?

EW WETNSIS YB UOR ROEHIBAV.

Answer: We witness by our behavior.

Review chapter 6 of this book if you want to learn the gospel better.

WHEN YOU

write a paper for school, you make sure that you have the facts straight, don't you? You might check the encyclopedia for facts, interview people, or read books that other people wrote. A good witness knows what he is talking about. You should always be ready to tell people about Jesus. But to be a good witness, you need to understand the gospel well enough to explain it to your friends.

God's Word

"The Holy Spirit will come to you. Then you will receive power. You will be my witnesses."
ACTS 1:8

We ask our God to help you live the good way that he called you to live. The goodness you have makes you want to do good, and the faith you have makes you work. We pray that with his power God will help you do these things more and more. We pray all this so that the name of our Lord Jesus Christ can have glory in you. And you can have glory in him. That glory comes from the grace of our God and the Lord Jesus Christ.
2 THESSALONIANS 1:11–12

Always be ready to answer everyone who asks you to explain about the hope you have. But answer in a gentle way and with respect.
1 PETER 3:15–16

What if I tell someone about Jesus and nothing happens?

Don't be discouraged if you tell someone the gospel and nothing happens. God is the One who opens people's hearts and minds so that the truth can get in. And He promises that His Word will do whatever He sends it to do. You can be sure that even when someone rejects the truth of the gospel, God will use your witnessing to do what He wants to do.

PRAYER STARTER

Dear God: Help me not to be discouraged when someone rejects the Good News.

WORD SCRAMBLE

Question: What should we *not* do when someone rejects the Good News?

EW DLOUHS TON EB RAGEDISCOUD.

Answer: We should not be discouraged.

What will you tell your friends about Jesus? Remember to keep the message simple enough for them to understand.

I'M SURE

that you've planted a seed and watched it grow. Sometimes when we share the gospel, it is like planting a seed. The seed needs to grow before it can produce fruit. Sometimes our witnessing is like watering seed someone else has planted. Sometimes it is like seed that is ready for harvest. When God's "seed" is ready, the person you witness to will believe in Christ for forgiveness and salvation. Your job is to keep planting as much seed as possible.

God's Word

I planted the seed of the teaching in you, and Apollos watered it. But God is the One who made the seed grow.
1 CORINTHIANS 3:6

There was a woman named Lydia from the city of Thyatira. Her job was selling purple cloth. She worshiped the true God. The Lord opened her mind to pay attention to what Paul was saying.
ACTS 16:14

"The words I say . . . will not return to me empty. They make the things happen that I want to happen. They succeed in doing what I send them to do."
ISAIAH 55:11

The story of the farmer and the seeds

Jesus used parables to teach the people truths about the kingdom of heaven. A parable is a story about common things that teaches a lesson about spiritual things.

One day Jesus told a parable about a farmer who went into his field to plant seed.

The farmer took handfuls of seed and scattered them everywhere he went. The seed he threw fell on four kinds of ground.

Some of the seed fell in the road. When the birds saw it, they came and ate it. So those plants never grew.

Some seed fell on ground that had a layer of rock just under the surface. Do you know what happened to that seed? It started to grow into plants . . .

But because the ground was rocky, there wasn't enough dirt for the plants to keep growing. So all of those plants died.

Some seed fell onto ground that had weeds. When that happened, the weeds choked out the seed. They kept the good plants from growing tall and strong.

God's Word

But some of the seed fell onto good ground. That seed grew into beautiful, healthy grain that the farmer could use for food.

In this story Jesus is comparing the seed the farmer plants to God's Word and how it grows in people's hearts.

Jesus used stories to teach . . . many things. He said: "A farmer went out to plant his seed. While he was planting, some seed fell by the road. The birds came and ate all that seed. Some seed fell on rocky ground, where there wasn't enough dirt. That seed grew very fast, because the ground was not deep. But when the sun rose, the plants dried up because they did not have deep roots. Some other seed fell among thorny weeds. The weeds grew and choked the good plants. Some other seed fell on good ground where it grew and became grain. Some plants made 100 times more grain. Other plants made 60 times more grain, and some made 30 times more grain. You people who hear me, listen!"

MATTHEW 13:3-9

How is sharing the Good News like planting seeds?

Sharing the Good News is like throwing seed. Sometimes it reaches people who are like good ground. The gospel takes root in their hearts and produces fruit in their lives.

Some people are like hard ground in the middle of a road. The seed lands on them, and it doesn't sink in. Then the devil comes and takes the seed away.

Other people are like rocky ground. The seed starts to grow, but it isn't strong enough. Those people act like believers, but they don't trust Jesus. When following Him becomes difficult, they turn away.

Some people are like weedy ground. Jesus is not really what they love most. And soon they turn away from Him.

The good ground stands for the person who hears the gospel, understands it, and believes in Jesus as Lord and Savior. The Word of God grows in them and produces spiritual fruit.

PRAYER STARTER

Dear God:
I want to be like the good ground.

WORD SCRAMBLE

Question: What happens when "seed" is thrown on good ground?

TI DUROPCES ARTLIPSIU RFIUT.

Answer: It produces spiritual fruit.

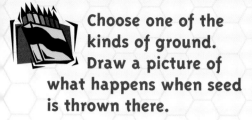

Choose one of the kinds of ground. Draw a picture of what happens when seed is thrown there.

Can you

imagine yourself as a kind of ground? Jesus' story tells what happens when we hear the Word of God. What kind of ground are you? What kind of ground do you want to be?

God's Word

"So listen to the meaning of that story about the farmer. What is the seed that fell by the road? That seed is like the person who hears the teaching about the kingdom but does not understand it."
MATTHEW 13:18-19

"And what is the seed that fell on rocky ground? That seed is like the person who hears the teaching and quickly accepts it with joy. But he does not let the teaching go deep into his life. He keeps it only a short time."
MATTHEW 13:20-21

"And what is the seed that fell among the thorny weeds? That seed is like the person who hears the teaching but lets worries about this life and love of money stop that teaching from growing."
MATTHEW 13:22

What if we aren't sure the person will listen?

When we share the gospel with someone, we usually cannot tell whether that person is like the good ground or the bad ground. But that shouldn't stop us from telling anyone about Jesus. Our job is to keep planting the seed everywhere we can.

If we keep spreading as much seed as possible, God will use what we do. He will use His Word to change people's lives. Only God can make the seed grow.

Jesus said the world is like a field that is ready for harvest. God has prepared much good ground that's ready for the gospel.

WORD SCRAMBLE

Question: What is the world like?

A DILEF DEARY ROF STARVEH

Answer: A field ready for harvest

Go out and tell everyone the Good News.

How many of your friends and neighbors don't know about Jesus? I'm sure you can think of more than just a few. There are many people in the world who have never even heard about Jesus and do not know that He can save them from sin. I hope you'll ask the Lord to use you as you tell other people about Jesus. And I hope you'll keep telling people about Him for the rest of your life.

God's Word

"I tell you, open your eyes. Look at the fields that are ready for harvesting now."
JOHN 4:35

"There are many people to harvest, but there are only a few workers to help harvest them. God owns the harvest. Pray to him that he will send more workers to help gather his harvest."
MATTHEW 9:37–38

Before people can trust in the Lord for help, they must believe in him. And before they can believe in the Lord, they must hear about him. And for them to hear about the Lord, someone must tell them.
ROMANS 10:14

CHAPTER 12

Heaven

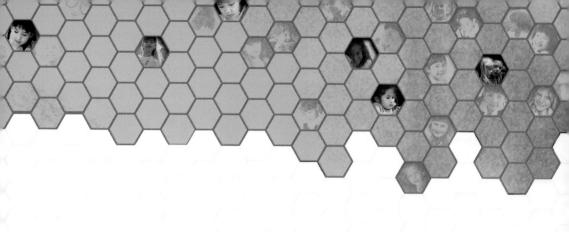

Where does God live?

God lives in a wonderful place called heaven. Jesus promised to take all real believers to live with Him there forever. He is getting heaven ready for us right now. Some day, when He is finished, Jesus will return for us. And He will take us to His beautiful home in heaven to live with Him forever.

WORD SCRAMBLE

Question: Who will live with Jesus forever?

LAL ALER LEEBEVIRS

Answer: All real believers

Find Jesus' promise about heaven in your Bible. It's in John 14.

God's Word

"There are many rooms in my Father's house. I would not tell you this if it were not true. I am going there to prepare a place for you. After I go and prepare a place for you, I will come back. Then I will take you to be with me so that you may be where I am."

JOHN 14:2-3

You may not always believe what your friends tell you. Sometimes you will know that what they say cannot be true. But you can *always* trust what Jesus said. We know He said, "There are many rooms in my Father's house. I would not tell you this if it were not true." So we know that there is plenty of room for all of us in heaven. And we know that Jesus wants us to live there with Him forever.

Is heaven the best place to live?

Do you remember that the Bible says God made the whole world, with all the stars and planets, in just six days? Can you imagine anything more awesome than that? Well, there is something more wonderful. It is heaven. Heaven is the most wonderful place God ever made. Jesus has been building our home in heaven for nearly two thousand years, and He is not finished with it yet. He will keep on building it until it is time for Him to come for us.

PRAYER STARTER

Dear God: Thank You for creating a place where I can be with You forever.

WORD SCRAMBLE

Question: Who is building our home in heaven?

SUSEJ SI BIDGUNIL RUO MHOE NI VAEHEN.

Answer: Jesus is building our home in heaven.

What do you think heaven is like? Write a story about it.

Have you

ever seen a really big house and wondered what it would be like to live there? The biggest house you can imagine is smaller than a tiny speck of sand compared to our home in heaven. Living there will be more wonderful than anything else. Everything in heaven will be perfect. Heaven is the best place to live, and we will live there forever.

God's Word

"In six days the Lord made everything. He made the sky, earth, sea and everything in them."
EXODUS 20:11

The Lord himself will come down from heaven. There will be a loud command with the voice of the archangel and with the trumpet call of God. And those who have died and were in Christ will rise first.
1 THESSALONIANS 4:16

You will teach me God's way to live. Being with you will fill me with joy. At your right hand I will find pleasure forever.
PSALM 16:11

SEE ALSO:
1 Corinthians 15:50-54

What is heaven like?

In heaven, everything will be new, and nothing will ever grow old. There will be no tears and no crying. There will be no sorrow, no sickness, and no death.

The Bible describes heaven as a place of very bright light. Everything there is like gold and precious jewels—very shiny and beautiful. There, will be no nighttime or darkness in heaven. There, nothing is bad or dangerous. There will be nothing but happiness in heaven.

WORD SCRAMBLE

Question: What is heaven filled with?

SINGHT ORF SU OT YENJO REFREVO

Answer: Things for us to enjoy forever

Write a poem or draw a picture of what you think heaven looks like.

WHaT are your favorite things to do?

Do you like to play sports or make music? Maybe you like to create art or write stories. God has made sure that heaven is filled with things for us to enjoy forever. Heaven will never be dull or boring. It will be much better than the best place you could ever imagine.

God's Word

The One who was sitting on the throne said, "Look! I am making everything new!"
REVELATION 21:5

"[God] will wipe away every tear from their eyes. There will be no more death, sadness, crying, or pain. All the old ways are gone."
REVELATION 21:4

The city was made of pure gold, as pure as glass. The foundation stones of the city walls had every kind of jewel in them.
REVELATION 21:18-19

The city's gates will never be shut on any day, because there is no night there.
REVELATION 21:25

What will people be like in heaven?

Everyone in heaven will love God and enjoy worshiping Him more than anything else. People in heaven will think about God all the time. For the first time ever, we will be able to love God with all our hearts. And enjoying Him will be our greatest pleasure. Heaven is a very happy place to be. It is a place where people will never be sad. They won't be bored or feel lonely. And they won't be sick.

WORD SCRAMBLE

Question: What will be our greatest pleasure in heaven?

YOJNEGIN HET DORL

Answer: Enjoying the Lord

In what way would you like to worship God in heaven? Practice doing it now. Sing a song or say a prayer. Create something special to tell God you love Him.

Do you know someone who has a physical disability? Perhaps you have a friend who uses a wheel-chair. Or maybe you know some-one who is sick all the time. We won't have our earthly bodies in heaven. We will have new, healthy bodies that never grow old or get sick. Everyone on earth who is hurt or sick will be well and whole in heaven. And they will stay that way forever!

God's Word

Also there are heavenly bodies and earthly bodies. But the beauty of the heavenly bodies is one kind. The beauty of the earthly bodies is another kind. The sun has one kind of beauty. The moon has another beauty, and the stars have another. And each star is different in its beauty. It is the same with the dead who are raised to life. The body that is "planted" will ruin and decay. But that body is raised to a life that cannot be destroyed.
1 CORINTHIANS 15:40–42

Our homeland is in heaven, and we are waiting for our Savior, the Lord Jesus Christ, to come from heaven. He will change our simple bodies and make them like his own glorious body. . . .
PHILIPPIANS 3:20–21

What did Ezekiel say about heaven?

Heaven is such a wonderful place that there are no earthly words to describe it.

When the prophet Ezekiel was allowed to see a little of heaven, he described an amazing scene. He saw something that looked like large, shining wheels within wheels. They had lights so beautiful that it was hard for Ezekiel to find words to tell about them. He described something like a large dome of sparkling ice and some wonderful creatures that were around the throne of God. Whatever he saw in heaven was certainly beautiful and amazing. Ezekiel was looking at the glory of God. I can't wait to see it for myself. Can you?

WORD SCRAMBLE

Question: What did Ezekiel see?

HET ROLYG FO ODG

PRAYER STARTER

Dear God: Thank You for creating a place so wonderful that I cannot even imagine it.

Draw a picture of what Ezekiel saw.

Have you

ever had a dream that seemed very real? The prophet Ezekiel had visions of God. He wasn't really dreaming. But while he was awake, the Lord allowed him to see a little bit of what heaven is like. Can you imagine how wonderful that was? God chose Ezekiel to see, and then Ezekiel wrote about it in his book in the Bible.

God's Word

I saw a wheel on the ground by each of the living creatures with its four faces. The wheels and the way they were made were like this: They looked like sparkling chrysolite. All four of them looked the same. The wheels looked like one wheel crossways inside another wheel. When they moved, they went in any one of the four directions. They did not turn as they went. I saw the rims of the wheels. The rims were full of eyes all around.
EZEKIEL 1:15–18

Now there was something like a dome over the heads of the living creatures. It sparkled like ice and was frightening.
EZEKIEL 1:22

What did John say about Heaven?

Ezekiel wasn't the only one who saw what heaven is like. Many years later, the apostle John also saw heaven. He said that an angel took him to see it. John described heaven like a very large city. Everything in that city is shining and beautiful. John also saw the glory of God, which is so bright that heaven needs no other light.

WORD SCRAMBLE

Question: What did John see?

A TUBFEALUI TYIC

Answer: A beautiful city

Draw a picture of what John saw.

Have you

ever seen anything made out of gold? Gold is very, very beautiful. Maybe you have seen jewels like sapphires and amethysts, or pictures of them. John said that the streets of the city were made of pure gold. The gold was as clear as glass. John also said that the walls of the city had every kind of jewel in them. Can you imagine anything more beautiful?

God's Word

This holy city is the new Jerusalem. It was prepared like a bride dressed for her husband. I heard a loud voice from the throne. The voice said, "Now God's home is with men. He will live with them, and they will be his people. God himself will be with them and will be their God."
REVELATION 21:2–3

The angel carried me away by the Spirit to a very large and high mountain. He showed me the holy city, Jerusalem. It was coming down out of heaven from God. It was shining with the glory of God. It was shining bright like a very expensive jewel, like a jasper. It was clear as crystal.
REVELATION 21:10–11

SEE ALSO:
Revelation 21:23–24

Will we all go to heaven?

All those who believe in and love Jesus go to heaven the very moment they die. As soon as they are gone from their bodies, they are in the presence of the Lord. Believers never have to be afraid of dying. Instead, we can look forward to living with Jesus Christ forever in God's perfect heaven.

WORD SCRAMBLE

Question: When will we go to heaven?

HET REVY NEMTOM EW IED

Answer: The very moment we die

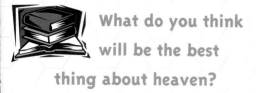

What do you think will be the best thing about heaven?

Have you

known anyone who has died? If that person believed in God, he went to heaven the second that he was gone from his body. You might miss that person very much. But you can be happy that he or she is with the Lord. Just imagine the beautiful things that person is seeing. There is happiness all the time. There is always something wonderful to do.

Someday we will all be together in heaven. Best of all, we will all be with the Lord. I look forward to being in heaven with Jesus forever. And I hope you do, too.

God's Word

We really want to be away from this body and be at home with the Lord.
2 CORINTHIANS 5:8

To me the only important thing about living is Christ. And even death would be profit for me. If I continue living in the body, I will be able to work for the Lord. But what should I choose—living or dying? I do not know. It is hard to choose between the two. I want to leave this life and be with Christ. That is much better.
PHILIPPIANS 1:21-23